CONCEPTS AND CHALLENGES

WATER AND AIR

Leonard Bernstein ◆ Martin Schachter ◆ Alan Winkler ◆ Stanley Wolfe

Stanley Wolfe
Project Coordinator

GLOBE FEARON
Pearson Learning Group

The following people have contributed to the development of this product:

Art and Design: Evelyn Bauer, Susan Brorein, Tracey Gerber, Bernadette Hruby, Carol Marie Kiernan, Mindy Klarman, Judy Mahoney, Karen Mancinelli, Elbaliz Mendez, April Okano, Dan Thomas, Jennifer Visco

Editorial: Stephanie P. Cahill, Gina Dalessio, Nija Dixon, Martha Feehan, Theresa McCarthy, Maurice Sabean, Marilyn Sarch, Maury Solomon, Jeffrey Wickersty, Shirley C. White, S. Adrienn Vegh-Soti

Manufacturing: Mark Cirillo, Tom Dunne

Marketing: Douglas Falk, Maureen Christensen

Production: Irene Belinsky, Linda Bierniak, Carlos Blas, Karen Edmonds, Cheryl Golding, Leslie Greenberg, Roxanne Knoll, Susan Levine, Cynthia Lynch, Jennifer Murphy, Lisa Svoronos, Susan Tamm

Publishing Operations: Carolyn Coyle, Thomas Daning, Richetta Lobban

Technology: Jessie Lin, Ellen Strain, Joanne Saito

About the Cover: All living things on Earth need water and air. About 75% of Earth's surface is covered with water. Clouds, such as the ones shown in the larger photograph, form when water vapor in the air condenses around tiny particles. When water in the colder air near the ground condenses, dew is formed. The leaves in the smaller photograph are covered with dew.

ISBN: 0-13-024201-2

Printed in the United States of America

1 2 3 4 5 6 7 8 9 10   06 05 04 03

1-800-321-3106
www.pearsonlearning.com

Acknowledgments

Science Consultants

Gregory L. Vogt, Ed.D.
Associate Professor
Colorado State University
Fort Collins, CO

Stephen T. Lofthouse
Pace University
New York, NY

Laboratory Consultants

Sean M. Devine
Science Teacher
Ridge High School
Basking Ridge, NJ

Vincent R. Dionisio
Science Teacher
Clifton High School
Clifton, NJ

Reading Consultant

Sharon Cook
Consultant
Leadership in Literacy

Internet Consultant

Janet M. Gaudino
Science Teacher
Montgomery Middle School
Skillman, NJ

ESL/ELL Consultant

Elizabeth Jimenez
Consultant
Pomona, CA

Content Reviewers

Sharon Danielsen (pp. 127–128)
Site Manager
Darrin Fresh Water Institute
Rensselaer Polytechnic Institute
Troy, NY

Art DeGaetano (Chs. 4, 5)
Associate Professor
Cornell University
Ithaca, NY

Dr. Nathan M. Reiss (Ch. 3)
Professor Emeritus
Department of Environmental Sciences
Rutgers University
New Brunswick, NJ

Dr. Gerald Schubert (Ch. 3)
Department of Earth and Space Sciences
University of California—Los Angeles
Los Angeles, CA

Dr. Dirk Schulze-Makuch (Chs. 1, 2)
Department of Geological Sciences
University of Texas at El Paso
El Paso, TX

Todd Woerner (pp. 76–77)
Department of Chemistry
Duke University
Durham, NC

Teacher Reviewers

Peggy L. Cook
Lakeworth Middle School
Lakeworth, FL

Claudia Toback
Consultant/Mentor
Staten Island, NY

Contents

Scientific Skills and Investigations Handbooks

Chapter *1* Inland Waters

Chapter *2* The Oceans

Features

Web InfoSearch

What are scientific skills?

People are naturally curious. They want to understand the world around them. They want to understand what causes earthquakes and where is the best place to search for useful minerals. The field of science would probably not exist if it were not for human curiosity about the natural world.

People also want to be able to make good guesses about the future. They want to be able to track severe storms such as hurricanes and to find ways to protect their homes against flooding.

Scientists use many skills to explore the world and gather information about it. These skills are called science process skills. Another name for them is science inquiry skills.

Science process skills allow you to think like a scientist. They help you identify problems and answer questions. Sometimes they help you solve problems. More often, they provide some possible answers and lead to more questions. In this book, you will use a variety of science process skills to understand the facts and theories in Earth science.

Science process skills are not only used in science. You compare prices when you shop and you observe what happens to foods when you cook them. You predict what the weather will be by looking at the sky. In fact, science process skills are really everyday life skills that have been adapted for problem solving in science.

1 NAME: What is the name for the skills scientists use to solve problems?

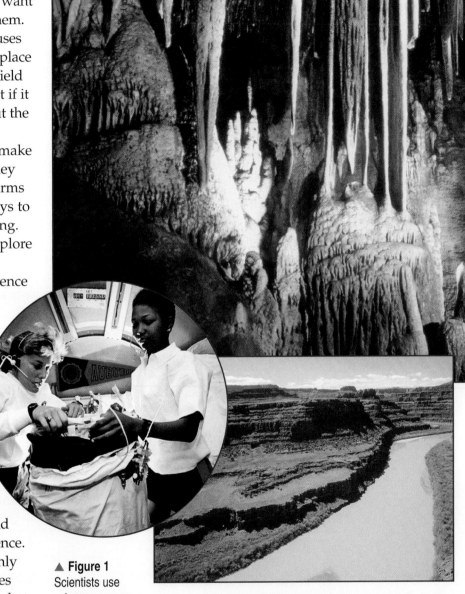

▲ **Figure 1**
Scientists use science process skills to understand how gravity affects the way crystals grow and materials mix, how caves form and change, how the land is built up and then torn down, and what Earth's place is in the universe.

Contents

1 Observing and Comparing

2 Classifying Data

3 Modeling and Simulating

4 Measuring

5 Analyzing Data and Communicating Results

6 Making Predictions

1 Observing and Comparing

Making Observations An important part of solving any problem is observing, or using your senses to find out what is going on around you. The five senses are sight, hearing, touch, smell, and taste. When you look at a pebble and feel its smoothness, you are observing. When you observe, you pay close attention to everything that happens around you.

Scientists observe the world in ways that other scientists can repeat. This is a goal of scientific observation. It is expected that when a scientist has made an observation, other people will be able to make the same observation.

▶ **LIST:** What are the five senses?

Comparing and Contrasting Part of observing is comparing and contrasting. When you compare data, you observe the characteristics of several things or events to see how they are alike. When you contrast data, you look for ways that similar things are different from one another.

▲ **Figure 2** River and glacial cut valleys look similar. However, you can see many differences from the valley floor.

▶ **COMPARE/CONTRAST:** How are valleys carved by running water and valleys carved by glaciers similar? How are they different?

Using Tools to Observe Sometimes an object is too small to see with your eyes alone. You need a special tool to help you make observations. One tool that scientists use to observe is the seismograph. A seismograph detects earthquakes by measuring the vibrations of Earth's crust.

▲ **Figure 3** Seismologist checking a seismograph

▶ **INFER:** Besides detecting earthquakes, what other use does a seismograph have?

Hands-On Activity
MAKING OBSERVATIONS

You and a partner will need 2 shoeboxes with lids, 2 rubber bands, and several small objects.

1. Place several small objects into the shoebox. Do not let your partner see what you put into the shoebox.
2. Cover the shoebox with the lid. Put a rubber band around the shoebox to keep the lid on.
3. Exchange shoeboxes with your partner.
4. Gently shake, turn, and rattle the shoebox.
5. Try to describe what is in the shoebox without opening it. Write your descriptions on a sheet of paper.

Practicing Your Skills

6. IDENTIFY: What science process skill did you use?
7. IDENTIFY: Which of your senses was most important to you?
8. ANALYZE: Direct observation is seeing something with your eyes or hearing it with your ears. Indirect observation involves using a model or past experience to make a guess about something. Which kind of observation did you use?

2 Classifying Data

Key Term

data: information you collect when you observe something

Collecting and Classifying Data The information you collect when you observe something is called **data.** The data from an experiment or from observations you have made are first recorded, or written down. Then, they are classified.

When you classify data, you group things together based on how they are alike. This information often comes from making comparisons as you observe. You may classify by size, shape, color, use, or any other important feature. Classifying data helps you recognize and understand the relationships between things. Classification makes studying large groups of things easier. For example, Earth scientists use classification to organize the different types of rocks and minerals.

▶ **5 EXPLAIN:** How can you classify data?

Hands-On Activity

ORGANIZING ROCKS

You will need 15 pebbles of different colors, textures, and shapes.

1. Lay the pebbles out on a table. Classify the pebbles into two categories based on texture: *Smooth* and *Rough.*

2. Look at the pebbles you classified as smooth. Divide these pebbles into new categories based on similar colors.

3. Repeat Step 2 for the pebbles you classified as rough.

Practicing Your Skills

4. **ANALYZE:** How did you classify the pebbles? What other ways could you classify the pebbles?

5. **EXPLAIN:** Why is a classification system useful?

3 Modeling and Simulating

Key Terms

model: tool scientists use to represent an object or process

simulation: computer model that usually shows a process

Modeling Sometimes things are too small to see with your eyes alone. Other times, an object is too large to see. You may need a model to help you examine the object. A **model** is a good way to show what a very small or a very large object looks like. A model can have more details than what may be seen with just your eyes. It can be used to represent a process or an object that is hard to explain with words. A model can be a three-dimensional picture, a drawing, a computer image, or a diagram.

▶ **6 DEFINE:** What is a model?

Simulating A **simulation** is a kind of model that shows a process. It is often done using a computer. You can use a simulation to predict the outcome of an experiment. Scientists use simulations to study everything from the insides of a volcano to the development of a tornado.

▲ **Figure 4** This student is discovering how volcanoes are created through successive layers of erupted lava.

▶ **7 DEFINE:** What is a simulation?

4 Measuring

Key Terms

unit: amount used to measure something

meter: basic unit of length or distance

mass: amount of matter in something

gram: basic unit of mass

volume: amount of space an object takes up

liter: basic unit of liquid volume

meniscus: curve at the surface of a liquid in a thin tube

temperature: measure of the amount of heat energy something contains

Two Systems of Measurement When you measure, you compare an unknown value with a known value using standard units. A **unit** is an amount used to measure something. The metric system is an international system of measurement. Examples of metric units are the gram, the kilometer, and the liter. In the United States, the English system and the metric system are both used. Examples of units in the English system are the pound, the foot, and the gallon.

There is also a more modern form of the metric system called SI. The letters *SI* stand for the French words *Système International*. Many of the units in the SI are the same as those in the metric system.

The metric and SI systems are both based on units of 10. This makes them easy to use. Each unit in these systems is ten times greater than the one before it. To show a change in the size of a unit, you add a prefix to the unit. The prefix tells you whether the unit is larger or smaller. For example, a centimeter is ten times bigger than a millimeter.

PREFIXES AND THEIR MEANINGS	
kilo-	one thousand (1,000)
hecto-	one hundred (100)
deca-	ten (10)
deci-	one-tenth (1/10)
centi-	one-hundredth (1/100)
milli-	one-thousandth (1/1,000)

◀ Figure 5

8 IDENTIFY: What are two measurement systems?

Units of Length Length is the distance from one point to another. In the metric system, the basic unit of length or distance is the **meter.** A meter is about the length from a doorknob to the floor. Longer distances, such as the distances between cities, are measured in kilometers. A kilometer is 1,000 meters. Centimeters and millimeters measure shorter distances. A centimeter is 1/100 of a meter. A millimeter is 1/1,000 of a meter. Figure 6 compares common units of length. It also shows the abbreviation for each unit.

SI/METRIC UNITS OF LENGTH	
1,000 millimeters (mm)	1 meter (m)
100 centimeters (cm)	1 meter
10 decimeters (dm)	1 meter
10 millimeters	1 centimeter
1,000 meters	1 kilometer (km)

▲ **Figure 6**

Length can be measured with a meter stick. A meter stick is 1 m long and is divided into 100 equal lengths by numbered lines. The distance between each of these lines is equal to 1 cm. Each centimeter is divided into ten equal parts. Each one of these parts is equal to 1 mm.

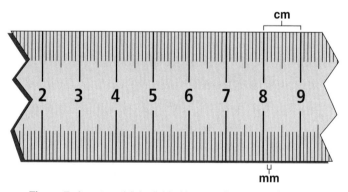

▲ **Figure 7** A meter stick is divided into centimeters and millimeters.

9 CALCULATE: How many centimeters are there in 3 m?

Measuring Area Do you know how people find the area of the floor of a room? They measure the length and the width of the room. Then, they multiply the two numbers. You can find the area of any rectangle by multiplying its length by its width. Area is expressed in square units, such as square meters (m^2) or square centimeters (cm^2).

> Area = length × width

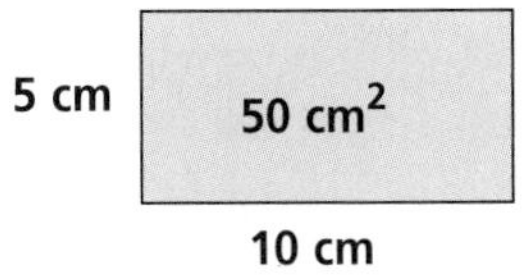

5 cm

50 cm²

10 cm

◀ **Figure 8** The area of a rectangle equals length times width.

▶ **10** **CALCULATE:** What is the area of a rectangle 2 cm × 3 cm?

Mass and Weight The amount of matter in something is its **mass.** The basic metric unit of mass is called a **gram (g).** A paper clip has about 1 g of mass. Mass is measured with an instrument called a balance. A balance works like a seesaw. It compares an unknown mass with a known mass.

One kind of balance that is commonly used to measure mass is a triple-beam balance. A triple-beam balance has a pan. The object being measured is placed on the pan. The balance also has three beams. Weights, called riders, are moved along each beam until the object on the pan is balanced. Each rider gives a reading in grams. The mass of the object is equal to the total readings of all three riders.

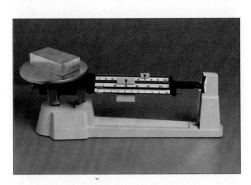

◀ **Figure 9**
A triple-beam balance

Mass and weight are related; however, they are not the same. The weight of an object is a measure of Earth's pull of gravity between Earth and that object. Gravity is the force that pulls objects toward the center of Earth. The strength of the pull of gravity between two objects depends on the distance between the objects and how much mass they each contain. So, the weight changes as its distance from the center of Earth changes.

▶ **11** **IDENTIFY:** What instrument is used to measure mass?

Volume The amount of space an object takes up is its **volume.** You can measure the volume of liquids and solids. Liquid volume is usually measured in **liters.** Soft drinks in the United States often come in 2-liter bottles.

A graduated cylinder is used to measure liquid volume. Graduated cylinders are calibrated, or marked off, at regular intervals. Look at Figure 10. It shows a graduated cylinder. On this graduated cylinder, each small line is equal to 0.05 mL. The longer lines mark off every 0.25 mL up to 5.00 mL. However, every graduated cylinder is not calibrated in this manner. They come in different sizes up to 2,000 mL, with different calibrations.

Always read the measurement at eye level. If you are using a glass graduated cylinder, you will need to read the mark on the graduated cylinder closest to the bottom of the meniscus. A **meniscus** is the curve at the surface of a liquid in a thin tube. A plastic graduated cylinder does not show a meniscus.

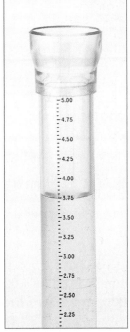

▲ **Figure 10** This glass graduated cylinder shows a meniscus.

The volume of solid objects is often measured in cubic centimeters. One cubic centimeter equals 1 milliliter (mL).

Look at Figure 11. Each side of the cube is 1 cm long. The volume of the cube is 1 cubic centimeter (cm^3). Now, look at the drawing of the box in Figure 12. Its length is 3 cm. Its width is 2 cm. Its height is 2 cm. The volume of the box can be found by multiplying length by width by height. In this case, volume equals $3 \times 2 \times 2$. Therefore, the volume of the box is 12 cm^3.

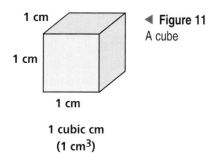

◄ **Figure 11**
A cube

1 cm
1 cm
1 cm

1 cubic cm
(1 cm^3)

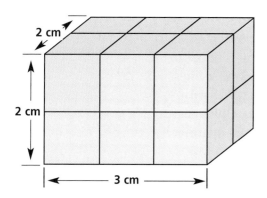

2 cm
2 cm
3 cm

▲ **Figure 12** The volume of a box equals length by width by height.

$$V = L \times W \times H$$

If you have a box that is 10 cm on each side, its volume would be 1,000 cm^3. A liter is the same as 1,000 cm^3. One liter of liquid will fill the box exactly.

12► CALCULATE: How many milliliters of water would fill a 12-cm^3 box?

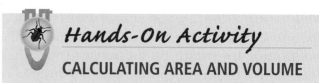

Hands-On Activity

CALCULATING AREA AND VOLUME

You will need 3 boxes of different sizes, paper, and a metric ruler.

1. Measure the length, width, and height of each box in centimeters. Record each measurement in your notes.

2. Calculate the volume of each box. Record each volume in your notes.

3. Find the surface area of each box. Record each area in your notes.

Practicing Your Skills

4. **ANALYZE:** Which of the three boxes has the largest volume?

5. **CALCULATE:** How many milliliters of liquid would fill each box?

6. **ANALYZE:** What is the surface area of the largest box?

Temperature **Temperature** is a measure of the amount of heat energy something contains. An instrument that measures temperature is called a thermometer.

Most thermometers are glass tubes. At the bottom of the tube is a wider part, called the bulb. The bulb is filled with liquid. Liquids that are often used include mercury, colored alcohol, or colored water. When heat is added, the liquid expands, or gets larger. It rises in the glass tube. When heat is taken away, the liquid contracts, or gets smaller. The liquid falls in the tube. On the side of the tube is a series of marks. You read the temperature by looking at the mark on the tube where the liquid stops.

Temperature can be measured on three different scales. These scales are the Fahrenheit (F) scale, the Celsius (C) scale, and the Kelvin (K) scale. The Fahrenheit scale is part of the English system of measurement. The Celsius scale is usually used in science. Almost all scientists, even in the United States, use the Celsius scale. Each unit on the Celsius scale is a degree Celsius (°C). The degree Celsius is the metric unit of temperature. Water freezes at 0°C. It boils at 100°C.

Scientists working with very low temperatures use the Kelvin scale. The Kelvin scale is part of the SI measurement system. It begins at absolute zero, or 0K. This number indicates, in theory at least, a total lack of heat.

COMPARING TEMPERATURE SCALES			
	Kelvin	Fahrenheit	Celsius
Boiling point of water	373K	212°F	100°C
Human body temperature	310K	98.6°F	37°C
Freezing point of water	273K	32°F	0°C
Absolute zero	0K	−459.67°F	−273.15°C

▲ Figure 13

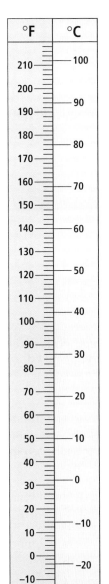

◀ Figure 14 The Fahrenheit and Celsius scales

Hands-On Activity

READING A THERMOMETER

You will need safety goggles, a lab apron, 2 beakers, a heat source, ice water, a wax pencil, a ruler, and a standard Celsius thermometer.

1. Boil some water in a beaker.
   ⚠CAUTION: Be very careful when working with heat. Place your thermometer in the beaker. Do not let the thermometer touch the sides or bottom of the beaker. Wait until the mercury rises as far as it will go. Record the temperature.

2. Fill a beaker with ice water. Place the unmarked thermometer into this beaker. Wait until the mercury goes as low as it will go. Record the temperature.

▲ **STEP 1** Record the temperature of the boiling water.

Practicing Your Skills

3. IDENTIFY: What is the temperature at which the mercury rose as high as it would go?

4. IDENTIFY: What is the temperature at which the mercury went as low as it would go?

13▶ NAME: What are the three scales used to measure temperature?

Handbook A: Developing Skills

5 Analyzing Data and Communicating Results

Key Term
communication: sharing information

Analyzing Data When you organize information, you put it in a logical order. In scientific experiments, it is important to organize your data. Data collected during an experiment are not very useful unless they are organized and easy to read. It is also important to organize your data if you plan to share the results of your experiment.

Scientists often organize information visually by using data tables, charts, graphs, and diagrams. By using tables, charts, graphs, and diagrams, scientists can display a lot of information in a small space. They also make it easier to compare and interpret data.

Tables are made up of rows and columns. Columns run up and down. Rows run from left to right. Tables usually show numerical data. Information in the table can be arranged in time order. It can also be set up to show patterns or trends. A table showing wind speed can reveal the effects the speed of wind will have on land. Figure 15 shows a table of gases in the atmosphere.

GASES IN THE ATMOSPHERE	
Gas	Percentage
Oxygen	21
Carbon dioxide	0.04
Nitrogen	78
Water vapor, helium, and other gases	0.02
Argon	0.94

▲ Figure 15

Graphs, such as bar graphs, line graphs, and circle graphs, often use special coloring, shading, or patterns to represent information. Keys indicate what the special markings represent. Line graphs have horizontal (x) and vertical (y) axes to indicate such things as time and quantities.

14▶ EXPLAIN: How do tables and graphs help you analyze data?

Sharing Results When you talk to a friend, you are communicating, or sharing information. If you write a letter or a report, you are also communicating but in a different way. Scientists communicate all the time. They communicate to share results, information, and opinions. They write books and magazine or newspaper articles. They may also create Web sites about their work. This is called written **communication.**

Graphs are a visual way to communicate. The circle graph in Figure 16 is showing the same information from Figure 15. The circle graph presents the information in a different way.

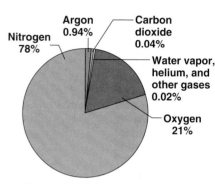

▲ **Figure 16** Circle graphs are a good way to show parts of a whole.

15▶ LIST: What are some ways to communicate the results of an experiment?

6 Making Predictions

Key Terms
infer: to form a conclusion

predict: to state ahead of time what you think is going to happen

Thinking of Possibilities When you **infer** something, you form a conclusion. This is called making an inference. Your conclusion will usually be based on observations or past experience. You may use logic to form your statement. Your statement might be supported by evidence and perhaps can be tested by an experiment. An inference is not a fact. It is only one possible explanation.

When you **predict,** you state ahead of time what you think will happen. Predictions about future events are based on inferences, evidence, or past experience. The two science process skills of inferring and predicting are very closely related.

16▶ CONTRAST: What is the difference between inferring and predicting?

How do you conduct a scientific investigation?

By now, you should have a good understanding of the science process skills. These skills are used to solve many science problems. There is also a basic procedure, or plan, that scientists usually follow when conducting investigations. Some people call this procedure the scientific method.

The scientific method is a series of steps that can serve as a guide to solving problems or answering questions. It uses many of the science process skills you know, such as observing and predicting.

Not all experiments use all of the steps in the scientific method. Some experiments follow all of them, but in a different order. In fact, there is no one right scientific method. Each problem is different. Some problems may require steps that another problem would not. However, most investigations will follow the same basic procedure.

▶ **1** DESCRIBE: What is the scientific method?

▲ **Figure 1** Scientists use the scientific method to guide experiments.

Contents

1 Identifying a Problem and Doing Research

Starting an Investigation Scientists often state a problem as a question. This is the first step in a scientific investigation. Most experiments begin by asking a scientific question. That is, they ask a question that can be answered by gathering evidence. This question is the reason for the scientific investigation. It also helps determine how the investigation will proceed.

Have you ever done background research for a science project? When you do this kind of research, you are looking for data that others have already obtained on the same subject. You can gather research by reading books, magazines, and newspapers, and by using the Internet to find out what other scientists have done. Doing research is the first step of gathering evidence for a scientific investigation.

▶ **IDENTIFY:** What is the first step of a scientific investigation?

BUILDING SCIENCE SKILLS

Researching Background Information Suppose you notice that a river running through your town looks brown on some days and clear on others. You also notice that when the river turns brown, it has usually rained the day before. You wonder if rain and the brown color of the river water are related.

To determine if the river water color is related to rainfall, look for information on rivers in encyclopedias, in geology books, and on the Internet. Put your findings in a report.

▲ **Figure 2** Water in river after a heavy rain.

2 Forming a Hypothesis

Key Terms

hypothesis: suggested answer to a question or problem

theory: set of hypotheses that have been supported by testing over and over again

Focusing the Investigation Scientists usually state clearly what they expect to find out in an investigation. This is called stating a hypothesis. A **hypothesis** is a suggested answer to a question or a solution to a problem. Stating a hypothesis helps to keep you focused on the problem and helps you decide what to test.

To form their hypotheses, scientists must think of possible explanations for a set of observations or they must suggest possible answers to a scientific question. One of those explanations becomes the hypothesis. In science, a hypothesis must include something that can be tested.

A hypothesis is more than just a guess. It must consider observations, past experiences, and previous knowledge. It is an inference turned into a statement that can be tested. A set of hypotheses that have been supported by testing over and over again by many scientists is called a **theory.** An example is the theory that explains how living things have evolved, or changed, over time.

A hypothesis can take the form of an "if…then" statement. A well-worded hypothesis is a guide for how to set up and perform an experiment.

▶ **DESCRIBE:** How does a scientist form a hypothesis?

BUILDING SCIENCE SKILLS

Developing a Hypothesis If you are testing how river water and rainfall are related, you might write down this hypothesis:

Runoff is one cause of the river water turning brown.

Your hypothesis is incomplete. It is not enough to link water color and rainfall. You need to explain what materials make the river water brown and how rainfall causes those materials to get into the water. Revise the hypothesis above to make it more specific.

3 Designing and Carrying Out an Experiment

Key Terms

variable: anything that can affect the outcome of an experiment

constant: something that does not change

controlled experiment: experiment in which all the conditions except one are kept constant

Testing the Hypothesis Scientists need to plan how to test their hypotheses. This means they must design an experiment. The plan must be a step-by-step procedure. It should include a record of any observations made or measurements taken.

All experiments must take variables into account. A **variable** is anything that can affect the outcome of an experiment. Room temperature, amount of sunlight, and water vapor in the air are just some of the many variables that could affect the outcome of an experiment.

▶ **4 DEFINE:** What is a variable?

Controlling the Experiment One of the variables in an experiment should be what you are testing. This is what you will change during the experiment. All other variables need to remain the same. In this experiment, you will vary the type of earth.

A **constant** is something that does not change. If there are no constants in your experiment, you will not be sure why you got the results you did. An experiment in which all the conditions except one are kept constant is called a **controlled experiment.**

Some experiments have two setups. In one setup, called the control, nothing is changed. In the other setup, the variable being tested is changed. Later, the control group can be compared with the other group to provide useful data.

▶ **5 EXPLAIN:** Explain how a controlled experiment is set up.

Designing the Procedure Suppose you now want to design an experiment to determine what makes river water brown. You have your hypothesis. You decide your procedure is to construct a slightly tilted model of the river, the town, and the land upstream from the town. You will send water down the river and measure the color and clarity of the water. Next, you will create artificial rain and again check the color and clarity of the water.

Does it matter how much rain you add to your model? Does it matter how heavy the rainfall is? Does 3 inches (7.5 cm) of rainfall in 5 minutes have the same effect on your model as 3 inches in 1 hour?

In designing your experiment, you need to identify the variables. The amount of water and the rate at which you apply it to your model are variables that could affect the outcome of your experiment. Another important variable for your experiment is the steepness of the river. To be sure of your results, you will have to conduct your experiment several times. Each time you will alter just one variable while keeping the other variables just the same.

Finally, you should decide on the data you will collect. How will you measure the color and clarity of the water of the river? You might make a color chart that you lower into the river water to see how the sediment in the water changes its color.

The hands-on activity on page 12 is an example of an experiment you might have designed.

◀ **Figure 3** In your experiment, you will elevate the trays with books to test soil runoff.

▶ **6 EXPLAIN:** How do constants and variables affect an experiment?

Hands-On Activity

CARRYING OUT AN EXPERIMENT

You will need 2 styrofoam meat trays from the grocery store, garden soil, grass sod, 2 plastic drinking glasses, 2 books, sprinkling can, scissors, and water. You should wear an apron and safety goggles.

1. Cut a small drain notch from the center of one end of each tray.
   ⚠ CAUTION: Be careful when using scissors.

2. Fill one tray with about a 1-inch layer (2.5 cm) of garden soil. Leave 2 inches (5 cm) of the notched end of the tray empty of soil.

3. Fill the second tray with a layer of sod except for 2 inches at the end with the notch.

4. Place the notched end of each tray at the edge of a table so that the trays extend over the edge a short distance.

5. Elevate the other end of the trays with books.

6. Label the cups Soil and Sod.

7. Sprinkle the soil tray with water. Keep sprinkling until the water runs off the surface of the soil and pours out the notch drain. Collect a glass of runoff water.

8. Repeat Step 7 with the sod tray.

Practicing Your Skills

9. **OBSERVE:** How much water did you have to sprinkle on the soil tray in order to collect a full glass?

10. **OBSERVE:** How much water did you have to sprinkle on the sod tray in order to collect a full glass?

11. **COMPARE:** Which glass had the dirtiest water?

12. **EXPLAIN:** What caused the difference in water clarity in the two cups?

13. **INFER:** What would be the best way to reduce soil runoff in rivers?

4 Recording and Analyzing Data

Dealing With Data During an experiment, you must keep careful notes about what you observe. For example, you might need to note how long the rain fell on the trays before water began running off. How fast did the water run off each tray? This is important information that might affect your conclusion.

At the end of an experiment, you will need to study the data to find any patterns. Much of the data you will deal with is written text such as a report or a summary of an experiment. However, scientific information is often a set of numbers or facts presented in other, more visual ways. These visual presentations make the information easier to understand. Tables, charts, and graphs, for instance, help you understand a collection of facts on a topic.

After your data have been organized, you need to ask what the data show. Do they support your hypothesis? Do they show something wrong in your experiment? Do you need to gather more data by performing another experiment?

 LIST: What are some ways to display data?

BUILDING SCIENCE SKILLS

Analyzing Data You made the following notes during your experiment. How would you display this information?

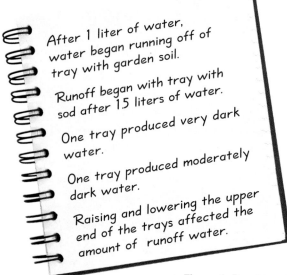

▲ **Figure 4** Possible notes

5 Stating a Conclusion

Drawing Conclusions A conclusion is a statement that sums up what you have learned from an experiment. When you draw a conclusion, you need to decide whether the data you collected supported your hypothesis. You may need to repeat an experiment several times before you can draw any conclusions from it. Conclusions often lead you to ask new questions and plan new experiments to answer them.

8 **EXPLAIN:** Why might it be necessary to repeat an experiment?

BUILDING SCIENCE SKILLS

Stating a Conclusion Review your hypothesis statement regarding the effect of surface material on rainwater runoff. Then, review the data you obtained during the experiment.

- Was your hypothesis correct? Use your observations to support your answer.
- Which surface reduced soil runoff better?

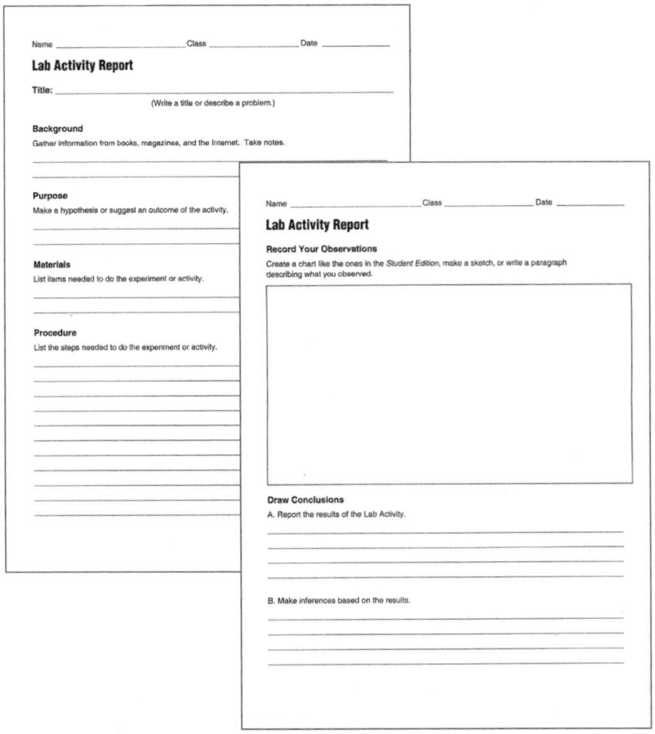

Name ______ Class ______ Date ______

Lab Activity Report

Title: ______
(Write a title or describe a problem.)

Background
Gather information from books, magazines, and the Internet. Take notes.

Purpose
Make a hypothesis or suggest an outcome of the activity.

Materials
List items needed to do the experiment or activity.

Procedure
List the steps needed to do the experiment or activity.

Name ______ Class ______ Date ______

Lab Activity Report

Record Your Observations
Create a chart like the ones in the *Student Edition*, make a sketch, or write a paragraph describing what you observed.

Draw Conclusions
A. Report the results of the Lab Activity.

B. Make inferences based on the results.

▲ **Figure 5** Throughout this program, you may use forms like these to organize your lab reports.

6 Writing a Report

Communicating Results Scientists keep careful written records of their observations and findings. These records are used to create a lab report. Lab reports are a form of written communication. They explain what happened in the experiment. A good lab report should be written so that anyone reading it can duplicate the experiment. It should contain the following information:

- A title
- A purpose
- Background information
- Your hypothesis
- Materials used
- Your step-by-step procedure
- Your observations
- Your recorded data
- Your analysis of the data
- Your conclusions

Your conclusions should relate back to the questions you asked in the "purpose" section of your report. Also, the report should not have any experimental errors that might have caused unexpected results. For example, did you follow the steps in the correct order? Did an unexpected variable interfere with your results? Was your equipment clean and in good working order? This explanation of possible errors should also be part of your conclusions.

9 **EXPLAIN:** Why is it important to explain possible errors in your lab report?

BUILDING SCIENCE SKILLS

Writing a Lab Report Write a lab report to communicate to other scientists your discoveries about soil runoff. Your lab report should include a title, your hypothesis statement, a list of materials you used, the procedure, your observations, and your conclusions. Try to include one table of data in your report.

LAB SAFETY

Working in a science laboratory can be both exciting and meaningful. However, you must always be aware of safety precautions when carrying out experiments. There are a few basic rules that should be followed in any science laboratory:

- Read all instructions carefully before the start of an experiment. Follow all instructions exactly and in the correct order.

- Check your equipment to make sure it is clean and working properly.

- Never taste, smell, or touch any substance in the lab that you are not told to do so. Never eat or drink anything in the lab. Do not chew gum.

- Never work alone. Tell a teacher at once if an accident occurs.

Experiments that use chemicals or heat can be dangerous. The following list of rules and symbols will help you avoid accidents. There are also rules about what to do if an accident does occur. Here are some rules to remember when working in a lab:

 1. Do not use glass that is chipped or metal objects with broken edges. Do not try to clean up broken glassware yourself. Notify your teacher if a piece of glassware is broken.

 2. Do not use electrical cords with loose plugs or frayed ends. Do not let electrical cords cross in front of working areas. Do not use electrical equipment near water.

 3. Be very careful when using sharp objects such as scissors, knives, or tweezers. Always cut in a direction away from your body.

 4. Be careful when you are using a heat source. Use proper equipment, such as tongs or a ringstand, when handling hot objects.

 5. Confine loose clothing and hair when working with an open flame. Be sure you know the location of the nearest fire extinguisher. Never reach across an open flame.

 6. Be careful when working with poisonous or toxic substances. Never mix chemicals without directions from your teacher. Remove any long jewelry that might hang down and end up in chemicals. Avoid touching your eyes or mouth when working with chemicals.

 7. Use extreme care when working with acids and bases. Never mix acids and bases without direction from your teacher. Never smell anything directly. Use caution when handling chemicals that produce fumes.

 8. Wear safety goggles, especially when working with an open flame, chemicals, and any liquids.

 9. Wear lab aprons when working with substances of any sort, especially chemicals.

 10. Use caution when handling or collecting plants. Some plants can be harmful if they are touched or eaten.

 11. Use caution when handling live animals. Some animals can injure you or spread disease. Handle all live animals as humanely as possible.

 12. Dispose of all equipment and materials properly. Keep your work area clean at all times.

 13. Always wash your hands thoroughly with soap and water after handling chemicals or live organisms.

 14. Follow the ⚠ CAUTION and safety symbols you see used throughout this book when doing labs or other activities.

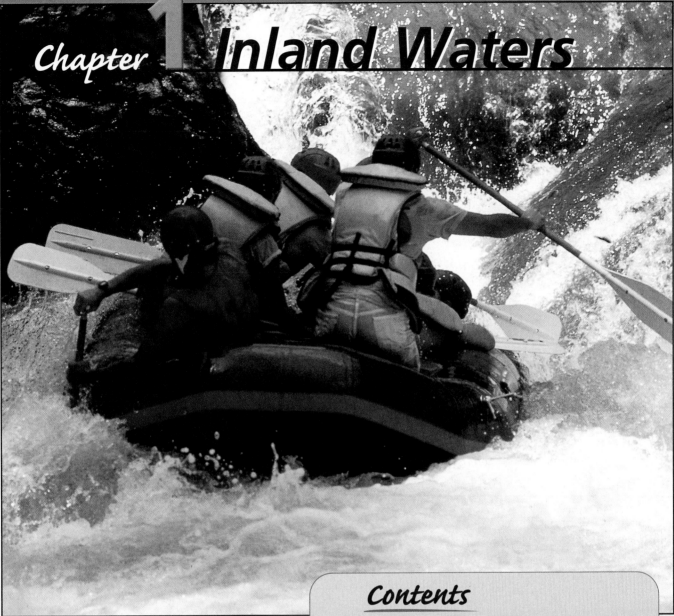

Chapter 1 Inland Waters

▲ **Figure 1-1** Riding the rapids is one way to explore rivers. It is also a fun pastime for many people.

Running water is important to people. It helps shape the land on which we live. We depend on rivers for transportation, farming, energy, and food. We also use rivers for recreational activities, such as boating and rafting. Many people enjoy riding the rapids. A rapid forms where a stream bed has a steep slope.

►How is running water important in transportation?

Contents

1-1 What is the water cycle?

Objective

Trace the steps in the water cycle.

Key Terms

evaporation (ee-vap-uh-RAY-shuhn): changing of a liquid to a gas

condensation (kahn-duhn-SAY-shuhn): changing of a gas to a liquid

precipitation (pree-sihp-uh-TAY-shuhn): water that falls to Earth's surface from the atmosphere

water cycle: repeated pattern of water movement between Earth and the atmosphere

Evaporation and Condensation Liquids change to gases by a process called **evaporation.** Most of Earth's surface is covered with water. When liquid water absorbs enough heat energy from the Sun, it changes into the gas water vapor. Air always contains some water vapor through evaporation. We become more aware of water vapor when the air is humid.

The changing of a gas to a liquid is called **condensation.** When air containing water vapor is cooled, the water vapor loses heat. If enough heat is lost, the water vapor changes to a liquid.

Water vapor condenses into tiny water droplets. These water droplets join to form clouds. If the temperature reaches freezing, ice forms. A cloud is a collection of water droplets or ice crystals.

1 **DESCRIBE:** What is a cloud?

Precipitation Water that falls to Earth from the atmosphere is called **precipitation.** Rain and snow are two forms of precipitation. As the water droplets in a cloud grow bigger, they become too heavy to stay in the air. Gravity pulls them toward Earth. The water falls as rain. If the rain passes through very cold air, the water may turn to a solid and fall to Earth as snow, hail, or sleet.

2 **LIST:** What are two forms of precipitation?

The Water Cycle Water is always changing state. As water evaporates from Earth's surface, it changes from a liquid to water vapor. In the atmosphere, the water vapor condenses to a liquid. This forms clouds. Finally, the water falls to Earth as precipitation. The repeated movement of water between Earth and the atmosphere is called the **water cycle.** The water cycle is also known as the hydrologic cycle.

About 97 percent of Earth's water is salt water. The rest is fresh water.

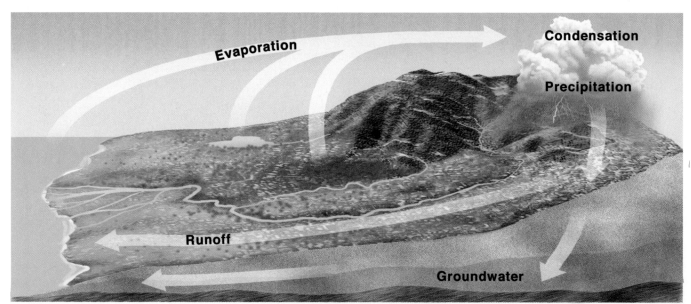

▲ **Figure 1-2** In the water cycle, water continually moves between the atmosphere and Earth.

About 76 percent of fresh water is frozen into ice caps near the North and South poles. A tiny amount is in the air in the form of water vapor. Only about 23 percent of Earth's fresh water is readily available for use by living things. That water is found in lakes, rivers, and streams, and below Earth's surface.

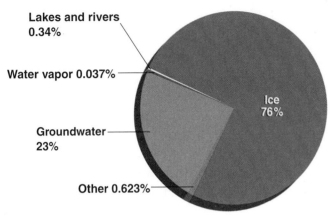

Lakes and rivers 0.34%
Water vapor 0.037%
Groundwater 23%
Other 0.623%
Ice 76%

▲ **Figure 1-3** Fresh water distribution on Earth

 STATE: What is the water cycle?

✓ CHECKING CONCEPTS

1. What happens when water absorbs enough heat?
2. During condensation, what happens to gas?
3. What makes up a cloud?
4. What processes make up the water cycle?

💡 THINKING CRITICALLY

5. **HYPOTHESIZE:** How might the water cycle be affected when dust in the air blocks sunlight?
6. **INTERPRET:** Based on Figure 1-3, what would you say is the largest source of fresh water available for use by living things?

BUILDING SCIENCE SKILLS

Classifying Write *Solid*, *Liquid*, and *Gas* across the top of a sheet of paper. Put each of the following terms under its correct state in your chart: rain, snow, water vapor, ocean, river, ice cap, and glacier.

Hands-On Activity

OBSERVING THE STATES OF WATER

You will need safety goggles, a glass, plastic wrap, a rubber band, hot water, and ice cubes.

1. Fill a glass halfway with hot tap water. Put a piece of plastic wrap tightly over the top of the glass. Use a rubber band to secure it. ⚠ CAUTION: Be careful not to burn yourself with the hot water.
2. Place 5 or 6 ice cubes on the plastic wrap as shown in Figure 1-4.
3. Allow the glass to stand for about 5 minutes. Observe what happens.
4. Pick up the plastic wrap. Feel the side that was closest to the hot water.

▲ **Figure 1-4** Set up your experiment as shown.

Practicing Your Skills

5. **IDENTIFY:** In what state was the hot water? The ice cubes? What state could not be seen?
6. **ANALYZE:** What happened to the ice? What caused this?
7. **ANALYZE:** What is on the underside of the plastic wrap? How did it get there?
8. **INFER:** Which state of matter are glaciers?

1-2 What is groundwater?

Objective
Explain how groundwater collects in soil.

Key Terms
pore: tiny hole or space

groundwater: water that collects in pores in soil and sinks into the ground

water table: upper layer of saturated rock and soil

Pores and Groundwater Some of the rain or snow that falls to Earth soaks into the soil. The water collects in the spaces, or **pores,** between bits of rock and soil. Water that collects between the bits of rock and soil and sinks into the ground is called **groundwater.** About 22 percent of Earth's freshwater supply is stored as groundwater.

1 DEFINE: What is groundwater?

Properties Affecting Groundwater Different kinds of rock and soil can hold different amounts of groundwater. Loosely packed rock or soil has many pores. It can hold a lot of groundwater.

Tightly packed rock or soil does not have many pores. It holds very little groundwater. Rock and soil containing particles that are all the same size can hold a lot of water. Suppose the soil particles are of all different sizes. Then, the smaller particles can fill up the pores. This kind of rock or soil has little room for water.

 2 DESCRIBE: When can rocks and soil hold a lot of groundwater?

Movement of Groundwater Groundwater moves easily through rocks and soil with large, connected pores. However, if the pores are not connected, the water cannot sink deeper into the ground.

3 DESCRIBE: How does groundwater travel?

The Water Table Groundwater eventually reaches bedrock, where it almost stops moving. The pores in the rock above begin to fill up. When the pores are completely filled, the rock or soil is saturated (SACH-uh-rayt-ihd). The underground water level rises. The upper layer of saturated soil and rock is called the **water table.**

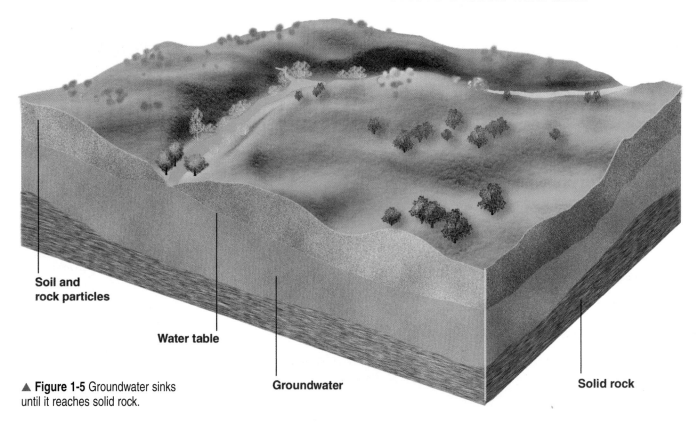

Soil and rock particles

Water table

Groundwater

Solid rock

▲ **Figure 1-5** Groundwater sinks until it reaches solid rock.

Because of the differences in soil density, not all of the water in the ground sinks down to the water table. Some of it stays near the surface, in the topsoil. Plant roots need this water because the roots of most plants do not reach the water table.

4 DEFINE: What is the water table?

✓ CHECKING CONCEPTS

1. Groundwater collects in _____ between soil particles.
2. About _____ percent of fresh water is stored as groundwater.
3. Loosely packed soil holds a lot of _____.
4. The upper layer of saturated rock forms the _____.

💡 THINKING CRITICALLY

5. INFER: Describe two ways in which your life would change if supplies of fresh water ran low.

INTERPRETING VISUALS

Use Figure 1-6 to answer the following question.

6. ANALYZE: Which soil sample can hold more groundwater, A or B? Why?

A
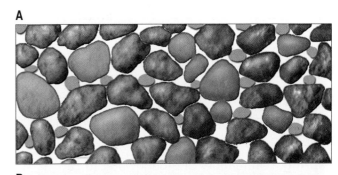

B
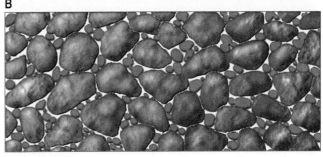

▲ Figure 1-6

People in Science

HYDROLOGIST

All living things need water to live. Water is also used for cooking, cleaning, bathing, and recreational activities. Industry and farming are dependent on water supplies.

Scientists who study Earth's water supplies are called hydrologists. Hydrologists work to keep us supplied with the fresh water we need. They may help select the best place to dig a well. They may draw up plans on how to route water from its source to a city. They help farmers irrigate their land by showing them how to use artificial canals or sprinkler systems. A hydrologist may also do research on how to keep water supplies clean. Many hydrologists work outdoors. A hydrologist must have a college degree and a background in geology, physics, chemistry, and mathematics.

▲ **Figure 1-7** A hydrologist searches in rock openings for groundwater sources.

Thinking Critically A developer is planning to build new homes with private wells. How could a hydrologist help this builder?

What are wells, springs, and geysers?

Objective
Describe how groundwater reaches Earth's surface.

Key Terms
well: hole dug below the water table that fills with groundwater

spring: natural flow of groundwater to Earth's surface

geyser (GY-zuhr)**:** heated groundwater that erupts onto Earth's surface

---

Wells In many places, people get their fresh water from wells. A **well** is a hole dug into the soil to reach below the water table. Water enters an opening in a pipe placed in the well. The water can then be pumped to the surface.

The level of the water table changes from season to season. When there is little rain, the level of the water table drops. The pipe for a well must be set much deeper than the water table line. This will ensure that the well will not run dry during dry weather.

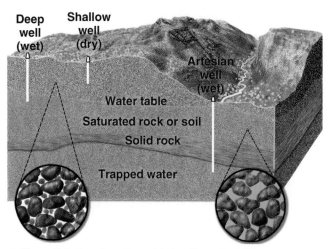

▲ **Figure 1-8** A well must reach below the water table.

▶ **DEFINE:** What is a well?

Artesian Wells A pump is not necessary to get water out of artesian (ahr-TEE-zhen) wells. Water rises freely from them.

The water level in an artesian well can rise higher than ground level. The water source, called a trapped aquifer, is under pressure. The pressure makes the water rise. An artesian well may be located far from its original water source.

▶ **EXPLAIN:** What makes water rise in an artesian well?

Springs A **spring** is a natural flow of groundwater that reaches Earth's surface. The side of a steep hill may dip below the water table. Water can then flow out of cracks in the rocks. This is why springs are usually found on hillsides. Spring water is often sold in stores as high-quality drinking water. Most spring water is cold. But when it is near an underground heat source, hot springs may form.

▶ **IDENTIFY:** Where are most springs found?

Geysers Sometimes steam and boiling water shoot into the air, forming a geyser. A **geyser** is heated groundwater that erupts onto Earth's surface. Water in a deep hot spring may be heated above the boiling point of water. If the water is trapped and pressure is generated, the water becomes superheated. This superheated water turns to steam. The pressure of the steam forces the water above it out into the air. Geothermal areas containing geysers are found in Wyoming, New Zealand, and Iceland, among other places.

▲ **Figure 1-9** This geyser, called Old Faithful, is found in Yellowstone National Park in Wyoming.

▶ **EXPLAIN:** What force causes geysers to erupt?

✓ CHECKING CONCEPTS

1. A well must be dug _____ than the water table.
2. Wells with no need for pumps are called _____ wells.
3. The temperature of spring water is usually _____.
4. Hot water erupting onto Earth's surface forms a _____.
5. Water heated above the boiling point is called _____ water.

💡 THINKING CRITICALLY

6. **INFER:** What states of water are found in geysers?
7. **HYPOTHESIZE:** Why does the temperature of spring water stay the same all year?
8. **INFER:** How is the hot water and steam found in hot springs and geysers used to generate electricity from geothermal energy?

Web InfoSearch

Oases An oasis is a very rich piece of land in the middle of a desert. Oases vary in size from less than 1 square kilometer to several square kilometers. The land for hundreds of kilometers around is dry and barren. However, an oasis has plenty of plant life and a natural spring. Many people live in oases.

SEARCH: Use the Internet to find out more about oases. Why do they have water? What is it like to live there? You can start your search at www.conceptsandchallenges.com. Some key search words are **desert oasis** and **geology.**

◄ **Figure 1-10** Oasis in an Egyptian desert

Hands-On Activity

MODELING GROUNDWATER USE

You will need gravel or aquarium stones, one aquarium tank, one small plastic tub, sandy soil, a watering can, and clean spray pumps from bottles.

1. Put a 7.5-cm layer of gravel or stones in the aquarium. Cover with a layer of sandy soil.
2. Using the watering can, let it rain on your aquarium until you have at least 5 cm of groundwater.
3. Insert the spray pump into the gravel. Start pumping into the plastic container. Record your observations. Note that if the soil is too sandy, it will clog your pump.
4. Add a few drops of food coloring to the watering can and water again. Repeat Step 3 and record your observations.

▲ **STEP 3** Pump the water into the plastic container.

Practicing Your Skills

5. **OBSERVE:** What happens to the water level as you pump?
6. **INFER:** How would adding food coloring to one water source affect the other?

1-4 What are rivers and streams?

Objective
Describe the three stages in the life cycle of a river or stream.

Key Terms
rapids: part of a river where the current is swift

waterfall: steep fall of water, as of a stream, from a height

meander (mee-AN-duhr)**:** loop in a mature river

oxbow lake: curved lake formed when a bend in a river is cut off at both ends

What Is a River? A river is a large, natural channel containing flowing water. River water flows downhill because of the force of gravity. The main sources of the water in the river are runoff from rainwater, streams that flow into the river, groundwater from springs, and melting snow.

▶ **1** DEFINE: What is a river?

The Stages of a River Rivers go through three stages in their development. The three stages can be described as youthful, mature, or old. However, the stage of a river is not really determined by the age of a river in years. It depends on how fast the water in the river flows and how steep the slope is that it is on.

▶ **2** IDENTIFY: What are the three stages in the development of a river?

Youthful Rivers A youthful river has a steep slope and fast-moving water. The Yellowstone River and the Niagara River are examples of youthful rivers. The fast-moving water erodes the riverbed, or bottom, and forms a narrow, V-shaped valley. The river fills almost the whole valley from side to side.

Two features of a youthful river are **rapids** and **waterfalls.** As the moving water rushes over steep slopes and rocks, rapids are formed. Sometimes the slope drops straight down. Then, a waterfall is formed.

▲ **Figure 1-11** Niagara Falls is a waterfall on the Niagara River.

▶ **3** INFER: What evidence indicates that the Niagara River is a young river?

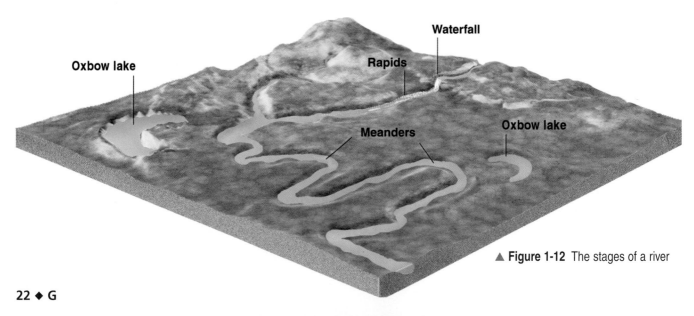

Oxbow lake

Waterfall

Rapids

Meanders

Oxbow lake

▲ **Figure 1-12** The stages of a river

Mature Rivers The waters of a mature river move slower than the waters of a youthful river do. A mature river is on a shallower slope. It does not have rapids and waterfalls. Erosion widens the river and the valley floor. This creates gentle slopes. The bottom is flatter. The sides are smoother and rounder. The river winds back and forth in loops called **meanders.** The Missouri River and the Ohio River are mature rivers.

 DEFINE: What are meanders?

Old Rivers Water moves very slowly in an old river. The Mississippi River is an old river. An old river has a nearly flat slope. Because of this, it floods easily. The slow river cannot get rid of the extra water, so it overflows.

▲ **Figure 1-13** A river floods its banks.

Flooding causes erosion and deposition along the meanders. Meanders do not extend to the valley walls. Over long periods of time, they change position. A meander may be cut off from the rest of the river. This forms a C-shaped lake called an **oxbow lake,** as shown in Figure 1-12.

 INFER: Why does an old river flow very slowly?

Endangered Rivers Rivers can be endangered. How? Mostly it is the pollution that results from developing new energy sources that endangers rivers. This includes building dams for power, draining acid from coal mines, and drilling for oil and natural gas resources. Since 1988, a report has been issued each year listing America's most endangered rivers. In 2001, the most endangered river on the list was the Missouri. Figure 1-14 lists endangered rivers from earlier years.

ENDANGERED RIVERS		
Year	River	Threat
2001	Missouri River	Dams
2000	Snake River	Dam operations
1999	Snake River	Dams
1998	Columbia River	Nuclear waste, irrigation of farmland
1997	Missouri River	Navigation
1996	Clarks Fork of Yellowstone	Proposed gold mine

▲ **Figure 1-14**

 EXPLAIN: What activities endanger a river?

✔ CHECKING CONCEPTS

1. Use the terms *youthful*, *mature*, or *old* to identify the stage of each river described: **a.** has a steep slope; **b.** has a nearly flat slope; **c.** forms oxbow lakes; **d.** has many rapids; **e.** has meanders.

💡 THINKING CRITICALLY

2. **EXPLAIN:** Why is a river with meanders sometimes said to "snake along"?

3. **PREDICT:** How can we tell if a lake near a river was once part of the river?

Web InfoSearch

The Nile River In the mid-1860s, the Royal Geographical Society sent the Scottish explorer Dr. David Livingstone to look for the source of the Nile River. Livingstone believed the source was Lake Tanganyika. He was gone a long time. No one heard from him. It was feared he was missing. A New York newspaper assigned Henry Morton Stanley, a journalist, to find him.

SEARCH: Use the Internet to find out more about this. What is the source of the Nile? Did Livingstone find it? What happened when Stanley finally met up with Livingstone? Start your search at www.conceptsandchallenges.com. Some key search words are **Nile River, Dr. David Livingstone,** and **H. M. Stanley.**

LAB ACTIVITY
Modeling the Life Cycle of a Stream

Materials

Safety goggles, lab apron, large plastic under-the-bed storage box, 2-liter soft drink bottle, two pieces of narrow aquarium hose (about 60 cm each), drill, waterproof cement, bucket, water, sand, funnel

BACKGROUND

Water in mountain streams moves very fast. It carries with it boulders, pebbles, and sand. These cause erosion. Downstream, water moves slower and has only enough force to carry silt. As streams erode the land, they become more winding and move more slowly. This is the typical life cycle of a stream.

PURPOSE

In this activity, you will study the development of a stream as it flows over sand.

PROCEDURE

1. Have your teacher drill a small hole in one end of the plastic box, near the bottom. This hole should be just large enough to put one piece of your aquarium tubing into it. Seal the hose around the hole with waterproof cement. This is your stream table.

2. Fill the tray evenly with sand about 6 cm deep. Shape the sand into a mound near the upper end. The other end should be almost free of sand.

3. Set the plastic box on a table. The end with the hole should be near the end of the table so that the hose can hang down. Put the catch bucket directly below the hose end. Raise the upper end of the box about 5 cm, using two or three textbooks.

4. Fill the plastic bottle almost full with water. Raise it about 12 cm by resting it on top of another large box or several large books. Put one end of the second piece of hose into the bottle.

5. Push the hose almost entirely under the water in the bottle so that the tube fills. Now, pinch off the free end of the hose.

▲ **STEP 3** Raise the upper end of the box about 5 cm.

▲ **STEP 4** Insert the second hose into the bottle.

▲ **STEP 6** Aim the water into the sand at the upper end of the stream table.

6. Let go of the pinched end, and the water will start flowing. Make sure this end is lower than the water level in the bottle. Aim the water into the sand at the upper end of the stream table. Remember to keep the other end of the tube in the water.

7. Keep adding water to the sand until it is saturated. You will know it is saturated when water begins to flow over the surface. Watch what happens to the water and sand as you let the water continue to flow for 15 minutes. Use the funnel to add water to the bottle as needed.

8. Copy the chart in Figure 1-15. In your chart, describe the appearance of the stream after 10 minutes. Also sketch the shape of the valley.

◀ **STEP 7** Watch what happens as water continues to flow over the sand.

Life Cycle of a Stream

	Appearance of stream	Valley sketches
Upper end		
Middle		
Lower end		

▲ **Figure 1-15** Use a copy of this chart to record your observations and draw your sketches.

CONCLUSIONS

1. **OBSERVE:** What happened to the sand when the water began flowing over it?
2. **OBSERVE:** What happened to the sand as it entered the "lake" at the lower end of the stream table?
3. **ANALYZE:** How does the stream change the land?
4. **INFER:** What will happen to the sand that ends up in a lake or an ocean?

1-5 What are lakes and ponds?

Objective
Describe how lakes and ponds form and how they change.

Key Terms
lake: low spot in Earth's surface filled with still water

pond: body of water similar to a lake but usually smaller and shallower

kettle lake: lake formed by a retreating glacier

reservoir: artificial lake

Still Waters Surface water that collects in hollows and low spots on Earth's continents forms **lakes** and **ponds.** Unlike the running waters of rivers and streams, lakes and ponds contain relatively still water. Ponds are similar to lakes but are usually smaller and shallower.

Well over 90 percent of the surface water on the continents is found in lakes. Most lakes contain fresh water. However, some of the largest lakes in the world are salty.

Like oceans, lakes have shorelines that erode. Many lakes are small enough to see across. Some lakes are so big that you cannot see the other side. Most of the water collected in lakes and ponds originally came from rain, snow, or melting ice.

1 DEFINE: What is a lake?

Formation of Lakes Low spots on Earth's surface are created in many ways, including erosion. Also, when glaciers receded from North America, big chunks of ice were left behind. These became covered by soil and slowly melted. The soil on top fell in, and large kettle-shaped depressions were formed. Water filled the kettles, making **kettle lakes.**

Land that shifts during earthquakes sometimes forms low spots that become lakes. Large rocks from space, called meteorites, have also caused holes that have later become lakes.

 DESCRIBE: How do lakes form?

Reservoirs Not all lakes are made by nature. People create lakes by building dams across rivers. A dam blocks the water until it reaches the top. The lake that is formed behind the dam is called a **reservoir.** As more water flows down the river, it is directed through a gate near the dam's top. The force of the running water can be used to power electric generators.

 DEFINE: What are reservoirs?

Growing Old Lakes and ponds change over long periods of time. Look at Figure 1-16 as an example. At their peak, ponds are clear pools of water. In time, sand, silt, and dead leaves and branches may fill in the bottom. The water near the shore can become very shallow, and many plants may start growing there. Eventually, the shoreline may become a marsh.

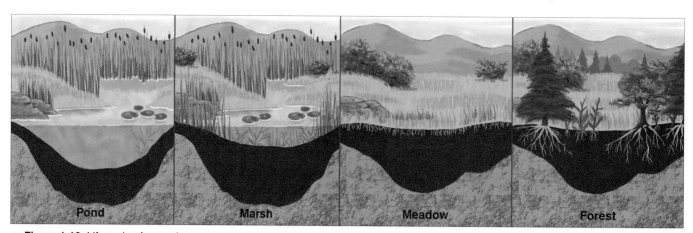

| Pond | Marsh | Meadow | Forest |

▲ **Figure 1-16** Life cycle of a pond

▲ **Figure 1-17** Lake George in New York State is fed by mountain streams and underground springs. It is a clear, deep lake with many fish and other wildlife.

When a pond is completely filled in, a meadow or a forest may grow on top. Only a slight dip in the land will show that a pond was once there. As old lakes and ponds fill in, new ones are being created elsewhere.

 DESCRIBE: How do lakes change over time?

✔ **CHECKING CONCEPTS**

1. Where does the water in lakes and ponds come from?
2. What can happen to a lake as it grows old?
3. How can people create artificial lakes?

 THINKING CRITICALLY

4. **INFER:** What happens to wildlife when a lake grows old?

DESIGNING AN EXPERIMENT

Design an experiment to solve the following problem. Include a hypothesis, variables, a procedure with materials, and a type of data to study. Also include a way to record the data.

PROBLEM: A river is bringing sediment from upstream into a dam. The engineers need to prevent the reservoir from filling with sediment. How can they stop the sediment from filling the dam's reservoir?

 Real-Life Science

FINDING FRESH WATER

You can see the Great Lakes in pictures of Earth taken from as far away as the Moon. The Great Lakes consist of five connected lakes along the border of the United States and Canada. The lakes are Superior, Michigan, Huron, Erie, and Ontario. Together, they contain a very large supply of fresh water. Scientists calculate that the five lakes combined hold 23,000,000,000,000,000 liters of fresh water. This is equal to about 20 percent of the world's total supply of fresh water. If this water were spread evenly over the United States, the country would be covered with almost 3 m of water.

▲ **Figure 1-18** Satellite image of the Great Lakes

The deepest Great Lake is Lake Superior. It averages 150 m deep. The shallowest is Lake Erie. It averages only 19 m deep. Water from the Great Lakes flows to the Atlantic Ocean. Niagara Falls connects Lake Ontario to Lake Erie.

Thinking Critically Cities around the country want to build pipelines to move Great Lake water to their growing communities. Do you think this is a good idea? Why or why not?

THE Big IDEA

Why are wetlands important to the environment?

How are swamps, bogs, and marshes alike? All are types of wetlands, or areas covered with shallow water.

For years, people thought that wetlands were simply a waste of good property. They drained the water and put down dry soil. Homes, roads, even shopping malls were then built on the newly landscaped areas. Almost half the original wetlands in the continental United States may have been destroyed in this way.

The destruction of wetlands has several harmful consequences. The chances for flooding increase. This is because wetlands act like giant sponges, soaking up runoff, groundwater, and precipitation. Another harmful result of wetland destruction is an increase in shoreline erosion. The roots of cordgrass and other saltwater plants commonly found in coastal wetlands anchor the soil. Without these natural anchors, bits of shoreline are broken off and carried away by waves.

Perhaps more importantly, filling in wetlands destroys the natural habitats of many plant and animal species. Inland wetlands are home to muskrats, beavers, and wood ducks. Coastal wetlands contain flounder, sea trout, and striped bass. They are also nurseries for many kinds of fish and crustaceans. Shrimp and crab populations are harmed every time a wetland is destroyed. Without wetlands, many of these animals could not survive.

Look at the illustrations on these two pages. Then, complete the Science Log to find out more about "the big idea." ✦

Mammals
Many mammals visit the wetlands regularly. Raccoons are mammals found throughout the United States, southern Canada, and Central and South America. Some types of raccoons live mainly on crabs they obtain from wetland areas.

Invertebrates
Crabs, worms, and clams are invertebrates that live in wetlands. They burrow in mud and are exposed as the water recedes during low tide. Invertebrates are animals that have no backbones. Because of their widespread diversity and abundance, invertebrates are an important part of many food webs.

Fishes

Many kinds of fish live in or visit the wetlands. Killifish is a common name for over 100 different species of fish. During high tide, some kinds of killifish swim into the marsh in search of food. Killifish are important in controlling mosquito populations.

Birds

Waterfowl such as the great blue heron stop at coastal marshes along their migratory routes. They use the ecosystem as a place to rest, feed, and breed.

Figure 1-19 More than one-third of threatened and endangered species in the United States live only in wetlands.

WRITING ACTIVITY

Science Log

Suppose your community was considering filling in a local wetland. How could this action affect the wildlife found in this wetland? How might this, in turn, affect the surrounding area? Do some research. Then, write an essay explaining why you think the wetland should or should not be destroyed. Start your search for information at www.conceptsandchallenges.com.

Chapter 1 Challenges

Chapter Summary

Lesson 1-1

- When liquid water takes in enough heat energy, it **evaporates,** or changes to a gas called water vapor. When water vapor loses enough heat, it **condenses,** or changes to a liquid.
- **Precipitation** is any form of water that falls from the atmosphere to Earth.
- The **water cycle** is the repeated movement of water between Earth and the atmosphere.

Lessons 1-2 and 1-3

- **Groundwater** collects in **pores** in soil. Soil with the same size particles can hold more groundwater than can soil with different-sized particles. Groundwater can move easily through soil with large, interconnected pores.
- The upper level of a layer of saturated rock is the **water table.** Some water remains near the surface of the soil.
- Groundwater can reach Earth's surface by means of a **well.** The level of the water table changes from season to season. Water rises freely out of an artesian well, so a pump is not needed.
- A **spring** is a natural flow of groundwater that reaches Earth's surface. Superheated groundwater breaks through to the surface as a **geyser.**

Lesson 1-4

- The three stages in the development of a river are described as youthful, mature, and old. A youthful river has a steep slope, fast-moving water, V-shaped valleys, and many rapids and waterfalls. A mature river has a shallower slope, is slow-moving, and forms **meanders.** An old river has a nearly flat slope and floods easily.

Lesson 1-5

- **Lakes** and **ponds** form in low areas of Earth's continents. The water in them comes mostly from rain, snow, or glacial ice and rivers and streams.
- A **reservoir** is an artificial lake.
- Lakes and ponds can age. This affects animals and plants that live in or near them.

Key Term Challenges

condensation (p. 16)
evaporation (p. 16)
geyser (p. 20)
groundwater (p. 18)
kettle lake (p. 26)
lake (p. 26)
meander (p. 22)
oxbow lake (p. 22)
pond (p. 26)

pore (p. 18)
precipitation (p. 16)
rapids (p. 22)
reservoir (p. 26)
spring (p. 20)
water cycle (p. 16)
waterfall (p. 22)
water table (p. 18)
well (p. 20)

MATCHING Write the Key Term from above that best matches each description.

1. tiny hole or space
2. upper layer of saturated rock and soil
3. bend in a mature river
4. low spot in Earth's surface filled with water from rain or snow
5. changing of a liquid to a gas
6. hole dug below the water table that fills with groundwater
7. heated groundwater that erupts onto Earth's surface
8. repeated pattern of water movement between Earth and the atmosphere

APPLYING DEFINITIONS Explain the difference between the words in each pair. Write your answers in complete sentences.

9. evaporation, condensation
10. precipitation, water cycle
11. spring, geyser
12. groundwater, well
13. lake, pond
14. kettle lake, oxbow lake
15. waterfalls, rapids

Content Challenges TEST PREP

MULTIPLE CHOICE **Write the letter of the term or phrase that best completes each statement.**

1. The process by which a gas changes to a liquid is called
   a. precipitation.
   b. evaporation.
   c. sublimation.
   d. condensation.

2. The main forms of precipitation are
   a. rain and sleet.
   b. sleet and hail.
   c. rain and hail.
   d. rain and snow.

3. About 23 percent of Earth's freshwater supply is stored
   a. as groundwater.
   b. in wells.
   c. in the oceans.
   d. in geysers.

4. In dry weather, the level of the water table in an area
   a. rises.
   b. drops.
   c. stays the same.
   d. increases, then decreases.

5. Old Faithful is
   a. a warm spring.
   b. an artesian well.
   c. a geyser.
   d. a hot spring.

6. The valley of a mature river is
   a. V-shaped with steep banks.
   b. V-shaped with gentle banks.
   c. narrow.
   d. steep.

7. The main threat to rivers is
   a. human recreation.
   b. overfishing.
   c. pollution.
   d. age.

8. A pump is usually used to get water from a
   a. geyser.
   b. spring.
   c. well.
   d. pond.

9. Artificial lakes are called
   a. reservoirs.
   b. oxbow lakes.
   c. kettle lakes.
   d. ponds.

10. Most of the fresh water that is found on Earth is found
    a. in groundwater.
    b. in lakes.
    c. in oceans.
    d. frozen in the polar ice caps.

FILL IN **Write the term or phrase that best completes each sentence.**

11. Water that evaporates from Earth and is changed to a gas is called _____.

12. A cloud is a collection of _____.

13. The pipe for a well should be _____ than the lowest level of the water table.

14. The temperature of spring water is usually _____.

15. A reservoir is a _____ created by a dam.

16. Like oceans, lakes have shorelines that _____.

17. The Yellowstone and Niagara rivers are _____ rivers.

18. Ponds are similar to lakes but are usually _____.

19. Glaciers help to form _____ lakes.

20. In 2001, the most endangered river in the United States was the _____ River.

Concept Challenges TEST PREP

WRITTEN RESPONSE **Answer each of the following questions in complete sentences.**

1. **CALCULATE:** If the level of a water table is 10 m below Earth's surface during the wet season and 15 m below the surface during the dry season, at what depth should a pipe for a well be placed? Why?

2. **CONTRAST:** How does a hot spring differ from a geyser?

3. **EXPLAIN:** How does a lake change over time?

4. **ANALYZE:** How can you tell the stage of a river by observing the shape of the river's valley?

5. **EXPLAIN:** How can a meander turn into an oxbow lake?

6. **ANALYZE:** How do plants get water if their roots do not go deep enough into the soil to reach the groundwater?

7. **HYPOTHESIZE:** How can people help rivers get off the endangered rivers list?

8. **HYPOTHESIZE:** What would happen to Earth's water supply if water did not evaporate?

INTERPRETING VISUALS **Use Figure 1-20 below to answer the following questions.**

9. Which letter in the diagram shows evaporation taking place?
10. What is evaporation?
11. Which letter in the diagram shows groundwater?
12. Where does groundwater come from?
13. Which letter in the diagram shows precipitation?
14. What are three other forms of precipitation?
15. Where does condensation take place?
16. What is condensation?

▲ Figure 1-20

Chapter 2 The Oceans

▲ **Figure 2-1** Coral reefs are home to a wide variety of life forms.

The oceans form the largest living environment on Earth. As on land, there are many smaller environments within the larger ocean environment. Coral reefs are an example. In addition to living things, the oceans contain valuable nonliving resources. They are great storehouses of dissolved minerals. For example, if all the water were evaporated from the oceans, a layer of salt about 50 m thick would cover the ocean floor.

▶ Coral reefs are often described as underwater rain forests. Why?

Contents

2-1 What is the world ocean?

Objectives

Describe the world ocean. Explain what is meant by oceanography.

Key Terms

world ocean: body of salt water covering much of Earth's surface

oceanography (oh-shuh-NAHG-ruh-fee): study of Earth's oceans

The Water Planet About 75 percent of Earth's surface is covered with water. Most of this is salt water. This large body of salt water is known as the **world ocean.** Earth is the only planet in the solar system that has a covering of liquid water.

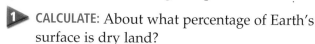 **CALCULATE:** About what percentage of Earth's surface is dry land?

Divisions of the World Ocean The world ocean is divided into three major bodies of salt water, also called oceans. These are the Atlantic Ocean, the Pacific Ocean, and the Indian Ocean. Geographers often mention two more oceans, the Arctic and the Antarctic. However, these are regarded by Earth scientists as parts of the Atlantic and Pacific oceans.

The word *sea* is sometimes used as another name for ocean. It also refers to a smaller body of water connected to or near an ocean.

Some inland bodies of water are also called seas. Most seas, though, are at least partly connected to an ocean. A gulf is a large area of ocean, larger than a bay, reaching into land.

▲ **Figure 2-2** Because of its great amounts of liquid water, Earth is often known as the blue planet.

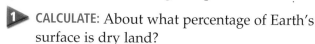 **IDENTIFY:** What are the three major oceans?

Size and Depth The Pacific Ocean is the largest of the world's oceans. More than half of Earth's ocean water is in the Pacific Ocean. The Pacific is also Earth's deepest ocean. Its average depth is 4.3 km.

The Atlantic Ocean is the second largest ocean. Several seas and gulfs are part of the Atlantic Ocean. Its average depth is 3.3 km.

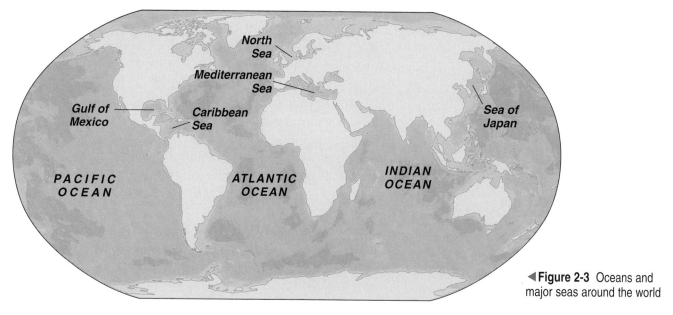

◀**Figure 2-3** Oceans and major seas around the world

North Sea

Mediterranean Sea

Gulf of Mexico

Caribbean Sea

Sea of Japan

PACIFIC OCEAN

ATLANTIC OCEAN

INDIAN OCEAN

The Indian Ocean is the smallest ocean. It is deeper than the Atlantic Ocean, but not as deep as the Pacific. The average depth of the Indian Ocean is 3.8 km.

 OBSERVE: Use Figure 2-3 to name two seas and a gulf that are part of the Atlantic Ocean.

Oceanography The study of Earth's oceans is called **oceanography.** Scientists who study the oceans and ocean life are called oceanographers. An oceanographer might specialize in the study of the oceans' depths, coral reefs, or the geography of the ocean floor.

 DEFINE: What is oceanography?

✔ CHECKING CONCEPTS

1. About how much of Earth's surface is covered with water?
2. How many oceans do geographers often name?

3. Which of Earth's oceans is the deepest?
4. About what fraction of Earth's ocean water is in the Pacific Ocean?
5. Why are Earth's oceans collectively called "the world ocean"?

THINKING CRITICALLY

6. **INFER:** Why is Earth often called the blue planet?
7. **HYPOTHESIZE:** Why would an oceanographer need to specialize?
8. **SEQUENCE:** List the three major oceans in order, from the smallest to the largest: Atlantic, Indian, Pacific.

BUILDING SCIENCE SKILLS

Graphing Create a bar graph that compares the relative depths of the three oceans.

 People in Science

MARINE BIOLOGIST

Marine biologists are oceanographers who study life in the ocean. They work in laboratories, aboard research ships at sea, or in coastal areas. If they work in the ocean, they must be in good physical shape. For example, they may dive into the deep ocean to observe the interactions of living things with the environment.

Research is a large part of marine biology. Some marine biologists take samples of ocean water to test the amount of pollution in it. They may investigate how the pollution affects sea life.

Research work is often done in special laboratories near the seacoasts. Among these laboratories are the Scripps Institution of Oceanography in California and

▲ **Figure 2-4** This marine biologist is studying manatees.

the Marine Biological Laboratory of the Woods Hole Oceanographic Institute in Massachusetts. Marine biologists must know biology, physics, chemistry, and math.

Some of the most exciting discoveries in marine biology have been made on the ocean floor. Deep-sea, or hydrothermal, vents are cracks in the ocean floor that leak hot, acidic water. The discovery of them gave marine biologists whole new communities of organisms to study.

Thinking Critically What tool would a marine biologist use to study ocean bacteria?

INVESTIGATE

Modeling Buoyancy in the Ocean
HANDS-ON ACTIVITY

STEP 3

You will need a drinking cup, soda water, and grapes.

1. Fill the cup almost full with the soda water.

2. Immediately add five grapes to the cup, one at a time.

3. Wait and watch.

THINK ABOUT IT: What physical force makes the grapes rise to the surface? What happens when the bubbles are knocked off the surface of the grapes? Why? How might this effect help underwater submersibles explore the deep ocean?

Objective

Describe three ways scientists explore the oceans.

Key Terms

sonar: echo-sounding system that bounces sound waves off the ocean floor

submersible (suhb-MUHR-suh-buhl)**:** underwater research vessel

Deep-Sea Drilling Samples of rock from the ocean floor can be obtained by drilling. Studying these samples allows scientists to learn more about the ocean floor. The Deep Sea Drilling Project (DSDP) was an important ocean research program that ended in 1983. The research ship *Glomar Challenger* was specially built for the DSDP. It could drill 4 km into the crust beneath the ocean. The DSDP was replaced in 1985 by another program called the Ocean Drilling Program (ODP). A new ship, called the *JOIDES Resolution,* took over for the retired *Glomar Challenger.*

▶ **EXPLAIN:** How do we get rock samples from the ocean floor?

Sonar Scientists can map the ocean floor by using sonar. The word *sonar* comes from the letters in <u>so</u>und <u>n</u>avigation <u>a</u>nd <u>r</u>anging. **Sonar** is an echo-sounding system. Sound waves travel through water at about 1,500 m/s. A transmitter bounces a sound wave off the ocean floor. The

returning sound wave, or echo, is picked up by a receiver. Scientists can measure the time it takes for the sound wave to return. This number can be used to calculate the depth of the ocean floor.

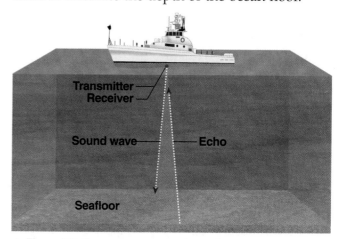

▲ **Figure 2-5** Sonar uses echoes of sound waves.

Suppose a sound wave makes a round trip in 10 seconds. The sound wave takes 5 seconds to reach the ocean floor. It takes another 5 seconds to bounce back to the ship. The depth of the ocean at that point is 1,500 m/s × 5 s = 7,500 m.

▶ **DESCRIBE:** What is sonar used for?

Submersibles Scientists also study the oceans by traveling in underwater research vessels called **submersibles.** One of the first submersibles to be developed was a bathysphere (BATH-ih-sfeer). The bathysphere remained attached to the research ship. Therefore, its movements were limited.

Another kind of submersible is called a bathyscaph (BATH-ih-skayf). A bathyscaph is not attached to anything. It can hold one pilot and two scientists. Scientists in the bathyscaph *Alvin* discovered many unusual forms of life in deep-sea vents. Robot submersibles equipped with underwater cameras can reach great depths and stay there for long periods of time.

▲ **Figure 2-6** This deep-diving minisub is a bathyscaph.

 EXPLAIN: How are robot submersibles better for deep-ocean research than other submersibles are?

✓ CHECKING CONCEPTS

1. What was the Deep Sea Drilling Project?
2. What does the word *sonar* stand for?
3. What is a submersible?

THINKING CRITICALLY

4. **CONTRAST:** How are a bathysphere and a bathyscaph different?
5. **CALCULATE:** A sonar signal sent out returns in 55 seconds. How deep is the ocean floor in that spot?

Web InfoSearch

Robot Submersibles Many submersibles have robots aboard. These can both explore and take pictures of the ocean floor. In 1985, Dr. Robert J. Ballard used the robot submersible *Argo* to find the remains of the sunken *Titanic*. On board was a robotic camera called Jason, Jr.

SEARCH: Use the Internet to find out more about these amazing vehicles. What else have they found in exploring the ocean floor? Start your search at www.conceptsandchallenges.com. Some key search words are **submersibles, underwater exploration,** *Titanic,* and **Robert Ballard.**

How Do They Know That?
PEOPLE CAN BREATHE IN THE OCEAN

People were not designed to breathe underwater. Yet, different devices have been invented to help us do just that.

In 1939, the self-contained underwater breathing apparatus, or scuba, was designed for use by the U.S. military. In 1943, two Frenchmen, Jacques Cousteau and Emile Gagnan, invented the Aqua-lung. This device allowed a diver both to breathe and to move about freely underwater. A tank filled with compressed air was strapped to a diver's back. A hose carried air from the tank to the diver's mouth. A valve controlled air flow. Cousteau tested the Aqua-lung in more than 500 dives. Aqua-lungs are still used today. In the 1950s, Cousteau built an underwater diving station at the edge of the continental shelf. Divers lived and worked there. Cousteau himself traveled all over the world exploring the oceans. He died in 1997. His granddaughter Alexandra continues his work.

▲ **Figure 2-7** A scuba diver can breathe underwater by using tanks filled with air.

Thinking Critically How did the Aqua-lung help in the study of the oceans?

2-3 What are some properties of the ocean?

INVESTIGATE

Testing the Density of Ocean Water
HANDS-ON ACTIVITY

1. Fill two 250-ml beakers or jars with 200 ml of tap water.

2. Add 3 tsp of salt to one beaker. Stir until the salt dissolves.

3. Place a whole, uncooked egg in each jar. Handle the eggs carefully to avoid breaking them. ⚠ CAUTION: Wash your hands when you are finished with this activity.

THINK ABOUT IT: What happened to the two eggs? What does this tell you about the difference between salt water and fresh water?

STEP 3

Objective

Explain why ocean temperatures and salinity in the oceans vary.

Key Terms

salinity (suh-LIHN-uh-tee): amount of dissolved salts in ocean water

thermocline (THUHR-muh-klyn): layer of ocean water in which the temperature drops sharply with depth

The Salty Sea The water in Earth's oceans is salt water. Salt water contains more dissolved salts and other minerals than fresh water does.

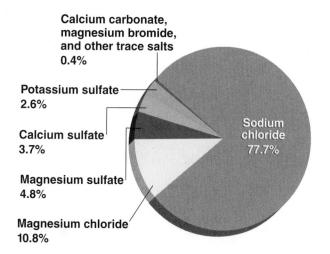

Calcium carbonate, magnesium bromide, and other trace salts 0.4%

Potassium sulfate 2.6%

Calcium sulfate 3.7%

Magnesium sulfate 4.8%

Magnesium chloride 10.8%

Sodium chloride 77.7%

▲ **Figure 2-8** Minerals in salt water

The amount of dissolved salts in ocean water is called **salinity.** Ocean water contains from 33 to 37 g of dissolved salt in every 1,000 g of water.

▶ **1 DEFINE:** What is salinity?

Levels of Salinity The salinity of ocean water differs slightly from place to place. Fresh water from rivers, precipitation, and melting glaciers lowers ocean salinity.

During the day, water evaporates from the surface of the ocean. Evaporation leaves behind dissolved salts. This raises salinity. Salinity varies more at the surface than in deep ocean water.

▶ **2 INFER:** Would rain increase or decrease the salinity in ocean water? Explain.

Temperature Layers Oceanographers recognize three "layers" of the ocean based on temperature. These layers are surface, thermocline, and deep.

Heat from the Sun warms ocean water. The water is warmest at the surface and coldest near the ocean floor. The surface layer is from 100 to 300 m deep. Constant winds and waves keep the water in the surface layer well mixed. As a result, the temperatures vary slightly in the ocean's surface layer.

Below the surface layer is the **thermocline.** In this layer, temperatures drop sharply with depth. The ocean below the thermocline, the deep layer, is even colder. Here the temperatures are usually below 5°C.

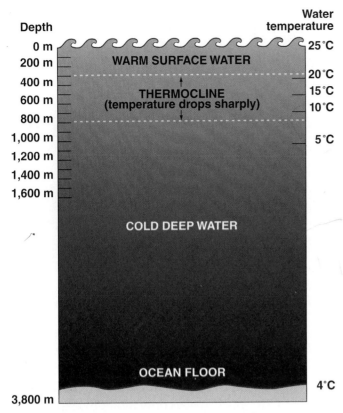

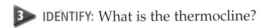

Depth | Water temperature

0 m — 25°C
200 m
WARM SURFACE WATER
400 m — 20°C
600 m — 15°C
THERMOCLINE
(temperature drops sharply)
— 10°C
800 m
1,000 m — 5°C
1,200 m
1,400 m
1,600 m

COLD DEEP WATER

OCEAN FLOOR — 4°C

3,800 m

▲ **Figure 2-9** Ocean temperature decreases as depth increases.

3 ▶ IDENTIFY: What is the thermocline?

Desalination Only a small part of Earth's fresh water is potable (POHT-uh-buhl), or fit to drink. Fresh water is a valuable natural resource that is in short supply.

As the population of the world increases, more fresh water is needed. Most supplies of fresh water depend on precipitation. During dry periods, those supplies are reduced.

Scientists have discovered a way to use ocean water to meet the increasing need for water. Before people can use the supply of water available in the ocean, minerals and salts in the ocean water must be removed.

In many places, desalination (dee-sal-uh-NAY-shuhn) plants have been built to remove the salts from ocean water. These plants use several different methods to remove salts. The most common is to heat the water until it evaporates, leaving the salts behind. The water vapor is then condensed to recover fresh water. Another method is to freeze ocean water. When ocean water is frozen, the ice formed is free of salts. The ice is then cleaned and melted to provide fresh water. Currently, Saudi Arabia, Israel, Malta, and some U.S. states operate desalination plants.

▲ **Figure 2-10** A desalination plant changes salt water into drinking water.

4 ▶ DESCRIBE: What happens when you desalinate water?

✓ CHECKING CONCEPTS

1. The amount of dissolved salts in ocean water is called _____.
2. Adding fresh water to salt water _____ the salinity of the water.
3. Ocean water is warmest at the _____.
4. There are _____ different temperature layers in the ocean.
5. Salinity varies more at the _____ than in deep ocean water.

💡 THINKING CRITICALLY

6. **SEQUENCE:** Use Figure 2-8 to list the minerals found in oceans, from the greatest percentage to the least.
7. **PREDICT:** The Mediterranean Sea has a high rate of evaporation. Would it have a high or low salinity? Explain.

BUILDING READING SKILLS

Vocabulary Write the definitions of the following words that contain the prefix *thermo*, meaning "heat": thermocline, thermoelectric, thermograph, thermomagnetic, and thermometer. Circle the part of the definition that relates to the prefix.

2-4 What are ocean currents?

STEP 3

INVESTIGATE

Comparing Densities of Cold and Warm Water
HANDS-ON ACTIVITY

1. Fill a plastic container half full with warm water. Wait for the water to stop moving.
2. Add several drops of food coloring to a cup of ice water and stir.
3. Using an eyedropper, gently dribble the colored water down the inside of the plastic container.

THINK ABOUT IT: What happened? Why? What does this tell you about the density of cold and warm water?

Objectives

Define current. Describe how surface currents and density currents are formed.

Key Terms

current: stream of water flowing in the oceans

Coriolis effect: bending of Earth's winds and ocean currents by Earth's rotation

density current: stream of water that moves up and down in ocean depths

On the Move The water in Earth's oceans is always moving. Have you ever heard of someone throwing a bottle containing a message into the ocean? Sometime later, the bottle is found far away.

How did it get there? It was carried by ocean currents. These **currents** are streams of water in the oceans. Some currents move along the ocean bottom. Some move up and down within the ocean depths. Currents can also flow along the surface.

1 DEFINE: What is a current?

Density Currents Differences in density can cause currents to move up and down in the ocean depths. This movement of water causes **density currents.**

Ocean currents can be warm or cold. Currents flowing from areas near the equator are warm. They bring warm water into cooler regions. These warm currents tend to warm the air over nearby land areas.

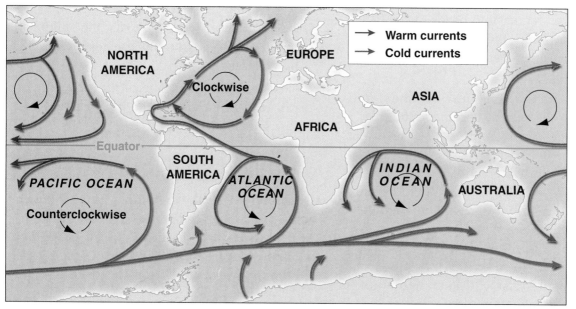

◀ Figure 2-11
Different densities in ocean water cause density currents.

Currents coming from areas near the poles are cold. They bring cold water into warmer regions and cool these areas. Cold water is denser than warm water. Cold water around the poles sinks to the ocean bottom. Water around the equator is warm. Warm water rises up toward the ocean surface.

Different amounts of salt in ocean water also cause density currents. Water with a lot of salt is denser than water with only a little salt. Dense, salty water sinks. Less salty water rises.

2 ▶ **DESCRIBE:** What conditions cause density currents in the ocean?

Surface Currents Winds cause most surface currents. Winds near the equator blow mainly from east to west. In the Northern Hemisphere, these winds blow from the northeast. In the Southern Hemisphere, these winds blow from the southeast. Earth's rotation causes the winds in the Northern Hemisphere to curve toward the west and the winds in the Southern Hemisphere to curve toward the east. This is called the **Coriolis effect.** Continents and large islands also influence ocean currents. As a result, surface currents move in huge circles. They move clockwise in the Northern Hemisphere and counterclockwise in the Southern Hemisphere.

3 ▶ **STATE:** What causes most surface currents?

☑ CHECKING CONCEPTS

1. Ocean currents are streams of _____ in the oceans.

2. Most surface currents are caused by _____.

3. Surface currents from the _____ are cold currents.

4. Surface currents from the _____ are warm currents.

💡 THINKING CRITICALLY

5. **HYPOTHESIZE:** Why do large land areas cause surface currents to change direction?

6. **COMPARE:** Which is probably denser, the water in the Arctic Ocean or the water in the Caribbean Sea? Explain your answer.

HEALTH AND SAFETY TIP

An undertow is a current that moves beneath and in a different direction from the surface current. Undertows can be very dangerous. This is one reason you should never swim alone. Interview a lifeguard to find out about other safety guidelines for swimming. Make a chart that outlines some of these guidelines.

Real-Life Science

TRAVELING ON CURRENTS

Knowing the direction and the strength of ocean currents is important to the shipping industry. Any good sailor knows that traveling with a current saves time.

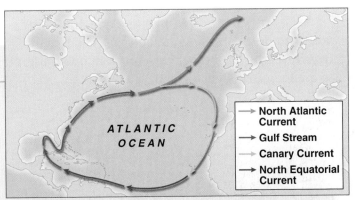

▲ **Figure 2-12** Currents can help ships cross the Atlantic Ocean faster.

In 1768, King George III asked Benjamin Franklin why it took mail ships longer to go from England to the colonies than to return to England. Franklin asked the captain of a whaling ship. He was told of a strong current of warm, salty water that flowed along the eastern coast of North America, then across the North Atlantic. Whaling ships rode the current going out but stayed outside of it when returning home. That ocean current is the Gulf Stream.

Thinking Critically How do you think ships today shorten their trip to Europe?

2-5 What are ocean waves?

Objective
Identify the properties of an ocean wave.

Key Terms
wave: regular up-and-down movement of water

crest: highest point of a wave

trough (TRAWF)**:** lowest point of a wave

How Waves Form When a wind blows across the water, waves are formed. A **wave** is a regular up-and-down movement of water. On a windy day at the beach, the ocean water gets rough. The waves are high when the wind is strong. On a calm day, the waves are not as high.

1▶ DEFINE: What is a wave?

Wave Shape A wave has a high point and a low point. The highest point, or top of a wave, is the **crest.** The lowest point of a wave is the **trough.** The height of a wave is the distance from crest to trough. Waves can reach heights of more than 15 m. However, eventually a wave reaches a point when it becomes too high and topples over. A white cap is then formed.

As you watch waves move across the water, you see one crest following another. The distance from one crest to another crest (or from one trough to another) is the wavelength of the wave.

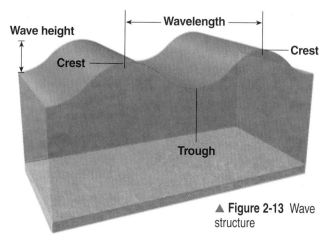

▲ **Figure 2-13** Wave structure

2▶ EXPLAIN: How is wave height measured?

Water Movement in Waves In deep water, the water in a wave does not move forward as the wave moves. Only the energy in the wave moves forward.

You can see the movement of water by watching a floating object. As a wave moves by, the object moves slightly forward. As the wave passes, the object falls back about the same distance. The object appears to be moving up and down in the same place.

As a wave moves across the ocean, water particles in the wave move in circles. At the surface, the size of the circles is the same as the height of the waves.

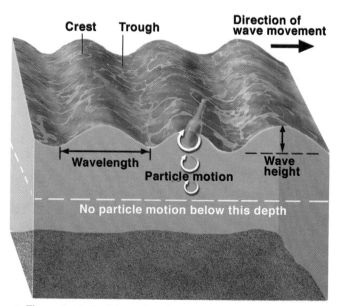

▲ **Figure 2-14** Particle motions in waves

3▶ DESCRIBE: How do water particles move in a wave?

Breaking Waves As waves move through deep water, they are not affected much by the depth of the water. However, the shallow waters of the shoreline drag on the wave and cause it to slow down.

As a wave slows down, its height rises until a certain critical height is reached. At this critical point, the wave breaks. The energy contained in the wave up until then changes form. The wave no longer moves in an up and down motion. It advances up the shore as a sheet of water.

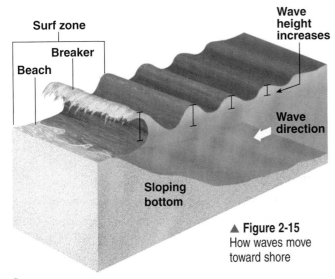

Surf zone
Breaker
Beach
Wave height increases
Wave direction
Sloping bottom

▲ **Figure 2-15**
How waves move toward shore

4 **EXPLAIN:** Why does a wave slow up in shallow water?

✓ CHECKING CONCEPTS

1. Most waves are caused by _____.
2. The top of a wave is the _____.
3. The distance between crests is the _____.
4. Only the _____ of a wave moves forward.

THINKING CRITICALLY

5. **MODEL:** Draw a wave and label it.
6. **INFER:** Early in the day, the water at the beach is fairly calm. Later in the day, the water begins to get rough. What do you think might be causing this?

Web InfoSearch

Tsunamis A tsunami (soo-NAH-mee) is an ocean wave. However, unlike other ocean waves, tsunamis are not caused by wind. Tsunamis carry a great deal of energy. They can be very destructive.

SEARCH: Use the Internet to find out more about tsunamis. What causes them? What happens as they approach the shore? To find out, start your search at www.conceptsandchallenges.com. Some key search words are **tsunamis, how tsunamis form,** and **underwater earthquakes.**

Hands-On Activity

MODELING WAVE MOTION

You will need an aquarium tank, metal washers, and four or five corks.

1. Fill the aquarium tank about 3/4 full of water.
2. Tie enough metal washers to a cork so that it floats about 3 cm from the tank bottom.
3. Repeat Step 2 with more corks so that they float 9 cm from the bottom, 15 cm from the bottom, and so on, until the last cork floats on the surface.
4. Make small, steady waves in the tank by moving your hand up and down in the water. Note what happens to each cork.
5. Repeat Step 4, but increase the height of the waves by moving your hand faster.

▲ **STEP 4** Make small, steady waves in the tank.

Practicing Your Skills

6. **ANALYZE:** How does increasing the wave height affect the motion of each cork?
7. **OBSERVE:** What features of a wave did you observe in this activity?

LAB ACTIVITY
Modeling the Shapes of Shorelines

Materials

Safety goggles
Lab aprons
Large plastic storage
    box
Water
Sand
Wooden paint sticks
Stopwatch or clock
Glue

BACKGROUND

Large waves carry great amounts of energy. Waves toss around rocks, sand, and swimmers. Gentle waves also contain energy that moves sand and finer particles around. Waves erode and shape shorelines.

PURPOSE

In this activity, you will study the development of a shoreline as it is struck by waves.

PROCEDURE FOR WATER-ONLY SHORELINE TABLE

1. Use the plastic storage box for the shoreline table. Set the shoreline table on a flat working surface. Raise one end of the box about 5 cm. Fill the box part way with water.

2. Create a wave generator by gluing together two paint sticks in a T-shape. Move the sticks back and forth in the water for a minute to create gentle waves.

3. Observe what happens to the waves as they approach shallower water. How do they change shape? Copy the first column only of the chart in Figure 2-16 and draw a picture of what you observe. Be sure to label your drawing.

4. Create more powerful waves and again observe what happens to the shoreline.

▲ **STEP 1** Raise one end of the storage box about 5 cm.

PROCEDURE FOR WATER AND SAND SHORELINE TABLE

5. Use the same plastic storage box for the next shoreline table. Set the shoreline table on a flat working surface. Raise one end of the box about 5 cm.

6. Fill the raised end of the shoreline table with sand that is 6 cm deep. Then, fill the box part way with water.

▲ **STEP 2** Move your wave generator around in the water.

7. Again, move the wooden paint sticks back and forth in the water to act as wave generators. Create gentle waves in your shoreline table.

8. Observe what happens to the sand on the shoreline as waves strike it. Copy the whole chart below and draw pictures of what you observe. Be sure to label your drawings.

9. Scoop out sand to make a small bay. Create waves for one minute and observe what happens to the bay. Draw what you see.

▲ **STEP 9** Create waves and draw how the bay looks now.

10. Place a small pile of sand in the middle of the shoreline to make a small peninsula. A peninsula is a land area that projects out into water.

11. Create waves for one minute and observe what happens to the peninsula. Draw what you see.

Waves and Shorelines		
Diagram of how waves change as they enter shallow water	Diagram of how waves changed the bay	Diagram of how waves changed the peninsula

▲ **Figure 2-16** Use a copy of this table on which to draw your diagrams.

CONCLUSIONS

1. **OBSERVE:** How did the waves change as they reached shallower water in the water-only shoreline table?

2. **OBSERVE:** What happened to the sand as waves broke on the shore of the water and sand shoreline table?

3. **ANALYZE:** How do waves change the shoreline?

4. **INFER:** What might happen to a shoreline that has both a bay and a peninsula?

2-6 What are the tides?

Objective
Describe what causes and affects the tides.

Key Terms
tide: regular change in the level of Earth's oceans
flood tide: incoming, or rising, tide
ebb tide: outgoing, or falling, tide

Ocean Water Levels   The water level of the ocean rises and falls throughout the day. Early in the day, ocean water rises and covers part of the beach. Later in the day, the ocean level falls. The beach is exposed. These regular changes in ocean water levels are called **tides.** A low water level is called low tide. A high water level is called high tide.

▲ **Figure 2-17** Low tide (above) and an incoming tide (below) in the same location

▶ DEFINE: What are tides?

Causes of Tides   You probably know that Earth's gravitational pull on the Moon keeps the Moon in orbit around us. But did you know that the Moon also pulls back on Earth and causes the tides? The Sun's gravitational pull also affects Earth's tides, but because it is so far away from us, not as strongly.

Earth's continents are slightly stretched by the pull of the Moon. Earth's oceans, which move more freely, are stretched even more. This stretching effect creates two bulges of water on Earth, one facing the Moon, the other directly opposite it. These bulges are the high tides. The bulging water also causes two areas with low tides between the high tides. As the Earth turns on its axis, the tide levels rise and fall.

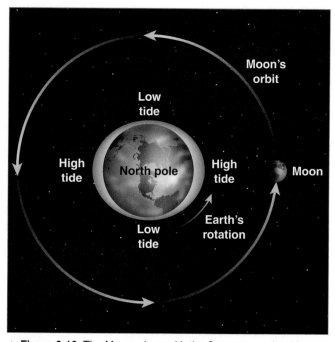

▲ **Figure 2-18** The Moon, along with the Sun, causes the tides. Whether it is high tide or low tide depends mostly on where you are on Earth relative to the Moon.

▶ IDENTIFY: What mainly causes tides on Earth?

Changing Tides   Some newspapers print tide tables. A tide table tells the times at which high tide and low tide will occur. If you look at a tide table, you will notice that it often shows two high tides and two low tides each day. The tides change about every 6 hours and 15 minutes.

TIDE TABLE

Sunday		Monday		Tuesday		Wednesday	
1 Low	4:45a	**2** Low	5:38a	**3** Low	6:27a	**4** Low	7:11a
High	11:31a	High	12:32p	High	1:25p	High	2:10p
Low	4:30p	Low	5:24p	Low	6:15p	Low	7:02p
High	10:24p	High	11:10p	High	11:55p		
8 Low	2:47a	**9** Low	3:31a	**10** Low	4:18a	**11** Low	5:10a
High	9:40a	High	10:13a	High	10:48a	High	11:23a
Low	4:26p	Low	4:58p	Low	5:30p	Low	6:05p
High	9:58p	High	10:46p	High	11:36p		

▲ **Figure 2-19** A newspaper gives the times for high and low tide.

Each quarter rotation of Earth causes a major change in tides. Water slowly floods the beach until high tide is reached. The incoming tide is called a **flood tide.** As Earth rotates another quarter turn, the water begins to leave the beach until low tide is reached. This outgoing tide is called an **ebb tide.**

 INFER: How often each day do flood tides occur?

 CHECKING CONCEPTS

1. What is the outgoing tide called?
2. What causes tides?
3. What is a flood tide?
4. How many times do the tides change each day?

THINKING CRITICALLY

5. **INFER:** Who would use a tide table? Why?
6. **PREDICT:** If low tide occurs at 6:30 A.M., when will the next low tide probably occur?
7. **HYPOTHESIZE:** Suppose you docked a boat where the tides rise and fall about 1 m. How would this affect the use of the boat?

INTERPRETING VISUALS

Use Figure 2-19 to answer the following question.

8. **INFER:** Fishing is best on mornings with high tides. Which day should you go?

 Real-Life Science

TIDES AND FISHING

Grunions are small silver fish that live in the Pacific Ocean off the coast of California. Grunions spawn and lay their eggs on sandy beaches from late February to early September, but only on nights of the highest tides. During this time, thousands of grunions cover the beaches. Many people gather on the beaches and catch the fish by hand. Some newspapers announce the nights the fish are expected to be on the beach.

Much of the fishing industry depends on an understanding of tides. Tides involve the movements of huge volumes of water. The water carries fresh oxygen. It also carries microorganisms, which serve as food for fish. Fish carried in with high tides can be easily trapped in nets later in the day.

▲ **Figure 2-20** Catching grunions on the beach is a common event in California.

The Bay of Fundy, between Nova Scotia and New Brunswick, Canada, is known worldwide for its tides. The difference between high and low tides can be over 10 m. This region is famous for its fishing industry.

Thinking Critically Why do you think the fish carried in with the high tides are easily trapped in the nets?

Objective

Describe different kinds of ocean sediments.

Key Terms

nodule (NAHJ-ool)**:** mineral lump found on the ocean floor

ooze: ocean sediment that contains the remains of many ocean organisms

Sediment Formation   Ocean sediments are formed by materials that collect on the ocean floor. Some sediments come from eroded land rocks. Others contain the remains of living things. Dust and ash from volcanoes sink to the ocean floor. Dust from space also falls and sinks to the ocean floor.

 LIST: What makes up ocean sediments?

Eroded Rock Sediments   Most of the sediments near the shore are eroded rock particles. Rivers carry rocks of all sizes to the ocean. Waves and wind also weather the rocks along the shoreline. These rock particles become ocean sediments. The sediments gradually spread out over the ocean floor. Large particles settle close to shore. Smaller particles settle farther from shore.

▲ **Figure 2-21** An arch can be formed by wind and waves eroding rock.

 EXPLAIN: What weathers rock to form sediment?

Nodules   Lumps of minerals called **nodules** are found on the ocean floor. Nodules form very slowly by a chemical process. Nodules are made up mostly of compounds of manganese, nickel, and iron. Small amounts of copper, lead, zinc, and silver are also found in ocean sediments. Most of the nodules lie thousands of meters deep in the ocean. Suction devices similar to huge vacuum cleaners have been used to collect them.

▲ **Figure 2-22** Nodules are lumps of minerals.

 DEFINE: What are nodules?

Ooze   Much of the ocean floor is made up of fine, soft sediments called **ooze.** At least 30 percent of ooze is the remains of ocean organisms. When ocean organisms die, their shells and skeletons sink to the ocean floor. These remains eventually fall apart or decompose. This material mixes with volcanic dust, clay, and water to form ooze.

▲ **Figure 2-23** Ooze may contain the decomposing skeletons of organisms such as these diatoms.

Much of the ooze on the ocean floor comes from tiny plants and animals such as the diatoms shown in Figure 2-23. Larger animals, such as clams and corals, also add to ooze.

 DEFINE: What is ooze?

Underwater Canyons Beyond the shoreline of the ocean, the land gradually slopes downward. Ocean sediments collect near the edges of these slopes. From time to time, the sediments slide down the slope, pushing water ahead of them. Gradually, this underwater landslide erodes the slope in places and forms canyons.

 IDENTIFY: What causes underwater landslides?

✓ CHECKING CONCEPTS

1. Fallen materials on the ocean floor form _____.

2. The largest rock particles settle _____ to shore.

3. Nodules are made up mostly of manganese, nickel, and _____.

4. Ooze is formed from _____.

5. Rocks are carried to the ocean by _____.

💡 THINKING CRITICALLY

6. **INFER:** Why do small rock particles settle farther from shore than larger rock particles do?

7. **INFER:** How do sediments from a volcano on land get into the ocean?

8. **EXPLAIN:** A large rock is located in a river. Outline the steps that might lead to this rock eventually breaking apart and being deposited as sediment on the ocean floor.

BUILDING SCIENCE SKILLS

Researching Find out about other kinds of ocean sediment. Then, make a chart listing them all. Add those discussed here. Say where they come from and what structures they form.

 Hands-On Activity

OBSERVING THE SETTLING OF OCEAN SEDIMENTS

You will need safety goggles, a plastic container with a lid, small pebbles, sand, soil, and water.

1. Place a small amount of pebbles, sand, and soil into a plastic container. Fill the container halfway with water. Then, put on the lid.

2. Shake the container gently for about 10 seconds.

3. Leave the particles undisturbed for several hours. Then, observe how the particles settled.

Practicing Your Skills

4. **OBSERVE:** Which particles settled on the bottom of the container? Which particles settled on top?

5. **ANALYZE:** Why did the particles settle out the way they did?

6. **COMPARE:** How is this like sediments settling out on the ocean floor?

▲ **STEP 2** Shake the container for 10 seconds.

Objective

Describe the ocean floor.

Key Terms

continental shelf: part of a continent that slopes gently away from the shoreline

continental slope: part of a continent between the continental shelf and the ocean floor

trench: deep canyon on the ocean floor

seamount: volcanic mountain on the ocean floor

guyot (GEE-oh): flat-topped underwater seamount

Continental Margin The continental margin divides a continent from the ocean floor. The edges of the continents extend into the oceans. At first, the continent slopes gently down under the ocean. This area is called the **continental shelf.** In some places, the continental shelf is very narrow. In other places, it extends for more than 150 km from the edge of the continent. Beyond the continental shelf is the **continental slope.** The continental slope is steeper than the continental shelf. It ends at the ocean floor.

▶ 1 COMPARE: Which is steeper, the continental shelf or the continental slope?

The Ocean Floor Like Earth's surface, the ocean floor has different landforms. The flat parts are plains. Plains cover about half of the ocean floor. High mountain ranges run along the middle of the oceans. These ranges are the mid-ocean ridges. In some places, mid-ocean ridges rise above the ocean surface to form islands.

▶ 2 IDENTIFY: What two landforms are on the ocean floor?

Trenches The ocean floor has deep **trenches**, or underwater canyons. The deepest of these is the Mariana Trench in the Pacific Ocean. This trench is more than 11,000 m deep. Mount Everest, the tallest mountain on land, is about 8,900 m high. Mount Everest could fit into the Mariana Trench and still be more than 2,000 m below the ocean's surface.

▶ 3 COMPARE: How does the depth of the Mariana Trench compare with the height of Mount Everest?

Seamounts and Guyots There are many mountains scattered around the ocean floor. These are called **seamounts.** Seamounts were once active underwater volcanoes. The ones that reach above the ocean surface form volcanic islands. The Hawaiian Islands are the peaks of underwater volcanoes.

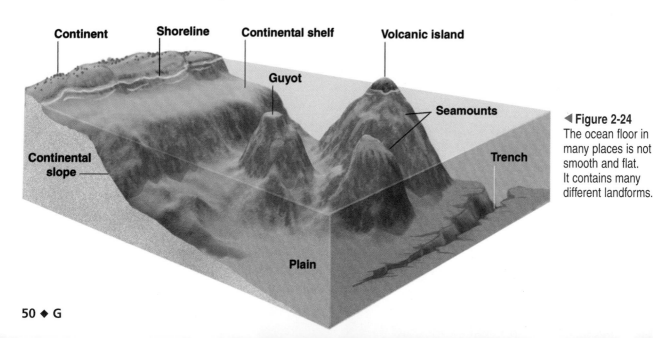

▶ Figure 2-24
The ocean floor in many places is not smooth and flat. It contains many different landforms.

Some underwater seamounts have flattened tops. These seamounts are called **guyots**.

 4 DEFINE: What is a guyot?

 ## ✓ CHECKING CONCEPTS

1. Two parts of the continental margin are the continental shelf and the continental _____.

2. Three landforms on the ocean floor are _____, mountains, and trenches.

3. Mountains on the ocean floor are called _____.

4. A _____ is an underwater seamount with a flat top.

💡 THINKING CRITICALLY

5. **PREDICT:** What would happen to the continental shelf if the sea level dropped sharply?

6. **HYPOTHESIZE:** On the ocean floor, mountains are higher and plains are flatter than they are on Earth's surface. Why do you think this is so?

Web InfoSearch

Fishing on the Grand Banks The most productive fishing grounds in the world are found on continental shelves. The Grand Banks off the east coast of Canada is an example. Fishing boats from Canada, the United States, Japan, and Europe catch tons of fish off the Grand Banks every year.

SEARCH: Use the Internet to find out more about the Grand Banks. What kinds of fish are found there? Start your search at www.conceptsandchallenges.com. Some key search words are **fishing, Grand Banks,** and **continental shelves.**

◀ **Figure 2-25** Fishing on the Grand Banks

How Do They Know That?

MAPPING THE OCEAN FLOOR

Much of the ocean floor cannot be seen from the surface. Until the twentieth century, the best method to map it was to tie a heavy object to a piece of rope and lower it into the water. The amount of rope used showed how deep the bottom was.

Certain technologies have made the ocean floor more visible to us. These technologies allow us to map it in great detail. The main advance in mapping occurred when sonar was developed in the 1920s. Modern sonar systems produce very detailed images.

Another advance was the camera sled. This device takes photographs of the ocean floor while it is being towed across it. For the mapping of small areas, submersibles are used. Also, satellites provide very precise measurements of seafloor features.

Thinking Critically What seafloor features does sonar map?

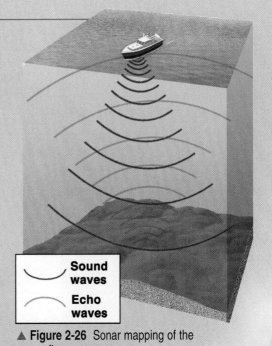

| Sound waves |
| Echo waves |

▲ **Figure 2-26** Sonar mapping of the ocean floor

2-9 What are coral reefs?

Objective

Describe three kinds of coral reefs.

Key Terms

coral: small animals found in warm, shallow ocean waters

fringing reef: coral reef that is directly attached to a shore

barrier reef: coral reef that forms around a sunken volcanic island

lagoon: shallow body of water between a reef and the mainland

atoll (A-tawl)**:** ring-shaped coral reef around a lagoon

Building the Reefs Tiny animals called **coral** live in warm, shallow ocean waters. The coral absorb calcium from the water. They use it to make hard skeletons of limestone, or calcium carbonate, around their bodies. Coral often attach themselves to other coral, forming a colony. New coral grow on top of dead ones. In time, a coral reef is formed.

◄ **Figure 2-27** A coral reef in Egypt's Red Sea. The pink-orange fish are basslets. Both the basslets and the soft coral are typical of Red Sea coral reefs.

▶ **DESCRIBE:** What is a coral reef made of?

Fringing Reefs and Barrier Reefs Two kinds of coral reefs are fringing reefs and barrier reefs. A **fringing reef** is a coral reef that is directly attached to a shore. It borders the coastline closely or is separated from it by only a narrow stretch of water. Fringing reefs are located along the east coast of Florida, among other places.

▲ **Figure 2-28** This fringing reef surrounds the South Pacific island of Bora Bora.

Barrier reefs form around sunken volcanic islands. The reef once extended out from the shore. As the island sank, the reef became separated from the mainland by a body of water. This body of water is a **lagoon.**

The Great Barrier Reef off the northeast coast of Australia is the world's largest barrier reef. It is more than 2,000 km long. In some places, it is almost 200 km wide. The Great Barrier Reef has been described by some as the largest structure ever built by living creatures. It actually consists of about 2,100 individual reefs and about 800 fringing reefs.

▶ **IDENTIFY:** Where do barrier reefs form?

Atolls A ring-shaped coral reef around a lagoon is called an **atoll.** An atoll forms around a sunken volcanic island. Only the circular coral reef remains above the ocean's surface. In the center of the atoll is the lagoon. Ships are sometimes able to enter the lagoons through channels that connect the ocean and the lagoon. Most atolls are in the Pacific Ocean.

▲ **Figure 2-29** Aerial view of Kayangel Atoll in the western Pacific Ocean

 DEFINE: What is an atoll?

CHECKING CONCEPTS

1. Where do the tiny animals known as corals live?
2. What do coral absorb from water to build reefs?

3. What is a reef colony?
4. What is found in the center of an atoll?
5. What are three kinds of coral reefs?

THINKING CRITICALLY

6. **COMPARE/CONTRAST:** How are fringing reefs and barrier reefs alike and different?
7. **INFER:** Why is the sand on a coral island white?
8. **HYPOTHESIZE:** Fossil coral reefs have been found beneath farmland far from the ocean. What might this discovery mean?

DESIGNING AN EXPERIMENT

Design an experiment to solve the following problem. Include a hypothesis, variables, a procedure with materials, and a type of data to study. Also include a way to record that data.

PROBLEM: Do the skeletons of coral contain calcium carbonate?

Integrating Environmental Science

TOPIC: ecosystems

ARTIFICIAL REEFS

Natural coral reefs support ecosystems. However, natural reefs take a long time to form. To help increase the fish population in the ocean, especially of those species used for food, people are building artificial reefs. These reefs also reduce beach erosion by blocking waves before they reach shore. The Japanese have been building artificial reefs for more than 300 years. The first artificial reef in the United States was built in 1830 off the coast of South Carolina.

Old oil rigs, old tires, sunken ships, concrete blocks, even old subway cars can serve as artificial reefs. Battle tanks and armored vehicles are part of a large artificial reef off the coast of Long Island in New York. Near Miami Beach, Florida, a 727 airliner was sunk to serve as a reef. Sea creatures such as coral, sea anemones (ah-NEM-oh-neez), mussels, barnacles, and sponges cling to or grow on the metal surfaces.

▲ **Figure 2-30** Artificial reefs can be built of almost anything, such as this sunken ship.

Thinking Critically How do reefs help increase the fish population?

THE Big IDEA

Where is life found in the ocean?

Many different kinds of organisms live in the ocean. Living things in the ocean are found in two main zones. The waters lying above the ocean bottom are called the pelagic zone. The waters next to the ocean floor are called the benthic zone.

Plankton are organisms that float along the surface of the pelagic zone. The motion of wind, waves, and currents moves these microscopic organisms. Some rise and fall in response to the day/night cycle.

There are two kinds of plankton. Phytoplankton (fyt-oh-PLANK-tuhn) are floating plantlike protists. These organisms use sunlight to make food from carbon dioxide and water. Phytoplankton are a source of food for floating animal-like protists called zooplankton.

Nekton are free-swimming ocean animals that move throughout the pelagic zone in search of food. Fishes, whales, dolphins, seals, and squids are nekton. Some nekton eat plankton. Others eat animals that have eaten plankton.

Organisms that live in the benthic zone are called benthos. Benthos are found in shallow waters along a coast and in the deepest parts of the ocean. Some benthos attach themselves to the ocean floor. They stay in that spot until they die. Mussels, barnacles, and some seaweeds are benthos that remain attached to the ocean floor. Some benthos bury themselves in sand or mud. Others, such as seastars and crabs, move around on the ocean bottom.

Look at the illustrations on these two pages. Then, complete the Science Log to learn more about "the big idea." ◆

Diatoms

Diatoms are one type of phytoplankton. When these single-celled organisms die, their glasslike shells sink to the ocean bottom, forming sediment.

Whales

Like all other mammals, whales have lungs and must come to the water surface to take in air. However, some whales, such as sperm whales, can dive to depths of 1,000 m in the pelagic zone.

Lanternfish and Angler Fish

Organs that give off light are located along the bodies of the lanternfish (shown in photo below). This adaptation helps the animal survive the cold, dark benthic zone. Female angler fish, which live on or near the ocean floor, have structures that look like fishing rods or lures on top of their heads to attract prey. The illustration shows two types of angler fish.

Dolphins

Just like other members of the whale family, dolphins are warm-blooded animals. Their body temperature stays about the same regardless of water temperature. Dolphins are strong swimmers and can dive to depths of 300 m.

Seastars

Seastars, also known as starfish, can grow a new arm if they lose one. They have tiny tube feet on their arms that help them move about the ocean floor. These organisms live in the shallow part of the benthic zone.

Mackerel

The streamlined body of a mackerel is adapted to swimming throughout the pelagic zone. Mackerel generally live and travel in large groups called shoals.

Science Log

Available sunlight, water depth, temperature, salinity, and seafloor sediments all influence how an ocean organism adapts to its environment. Choose a marine organism. Research how its environment relates to how it lives. Write a report to be sent to an agency that monitors the environment, such as the Environmental Protection Agency (EPA). Start your search at www.conceptsandchallenges.com.

Figure 2-31 Sunlight and water temperature decrease as you move from the pelagic zone down to the benthic zone of the ocean. This affects the kinds of ocean life that live there.

Chapter 2 Challenges

Chapter Summary

Lessons 2-1 and 2-2

- The world ocean is divided into three major oceans. The Pacific is the largest. The Atlantic is the second largest. The Indian is the smallest.
- Oceanographers use small **submersibles, sonar,** and ocean cores from drilling to study the oceans.

Lesson 2-3

- Salt water contains many more dissolved salts and other minerals than fresh water does.
- The ocean has three different temperature layers. In the **thermocline,** the temperature drops sharply.

Lessons 2-4, 2-5, and 2-6

- **Currents** of water move through the oceans. Most surface currents are caused by wind. They move in different directions in each hemisphere. Ocean currents can be warm or cold. **Density currents** move up and down in the ocean depths.
- Waves are formed by wind. They have **crests** and **troughs.**
- Only the energy, not the water, in a wave moves forward. Waves form breakers near the shore.
- High and low tides change the ocean's surface level. They are caused mostly by the Moon's gravity. **Flood tides** and **ebb tides** are caused by the rotation of Earth.

Lesson 2-7

- Eroded rock particles form most of the sediments close to shore. Minerals also help form ocean sediments.
- Much of the ocean floor is made up of **ooze.**

Lessons 2-8 and 2-9

- The **continental shelf** and **continental slope** lead into the ocean floor. Deep canyons, or **trenches,** are found on the floor. The flat parts of the ocean floor are called plains.
- **Seamounts** are underwater volcanoes and mountains. A **guyot** is a flattened seamount.
- A coral reef is made up of the skeletons of living and dead **coral. Fringing reefs** are attached to a coastline. **Barrier reefs** form around partially sunken volcanic islands. **Atolls** are ring-shaped coral reefs around **lagoons.**

Key Term Challenges

atoll (p. 52)
barrier reef (p. 52)
continental shelf (p. 50)
continental slope (p. 50)
coral (p. 52)
Coriolis effect (p. 40)
crest (p. 42)
current (p. 40)
density current (p. 40)
ebb tide (p. 46)
flood tide (p. 46)
fringing reef (p. 52)
guyot (p. 50)
lagoon (p. 52)
nodule (p. 48)
oceanography (p. 34)
ooze (p. 48)
salinity (p. 38)
seamount (p. 50)
sonar (p. 36)
submersible (p. 36)
thermocline (p. 38)
tide (p. 46)
trench (p. 50)
trough (p. 42)
wave (p. 42)
world ocean (p. 34)

MATCHING **Write the Key Term from above that best matches each description.**

1. study of Earth's oceans
2. underwater research vessel
3. amount of dissolved salts and minerals in ocean water
4. layer of ocean water in which temperature drops sharply
5. stream of water flowing in the ocean
6. regular up and down movement of water at the surface
7. stream of water that moves up and down in the ocean's depths
8. mineral lump found on the ocean floor
9. kind of ocean sediment
10. deep canyon on the ocean floor

APPLYING DEFINITIONS **Explain the difference between the words in each pair. Write your answers in complete sentences.**

11. crest, trough
12. continental shelf, continental slope
13. seamount, guyot
14. coral, atoll
15. lagoon, sea
16. barrier reef, fringing reef

Content Challenges TEST PREP

MULTIPLE CHOICE **Write the letter of the term or phrase that best completes each statement.**

1. The three major oceans are the
   a. Indian, Atlantic, Pacific.
   b. Pacific, Antarctic, Indian.
   c. Arctic, Pacific, Indian.
   d. Atlantic, Pacific, Caribbean.

2. The study of the world's oceans is called
   a. hydrology.
   b. geography.
   c. oceanography.
   d. technology.

3. To find the depth of the ocean, scientists use
   a. hydrology.
   b. sonar.
   c. bathyspheres.
   d. bathyscaphs.

4. Ocean water is warmest
   a. at the surface.
   b. in the thermocline.
   c. in the deep ocean.
   d. at the continental margin.

5. Warm ocean currents come from areas near the
   a. North Pole.
   b. South Pole.
   c. prime meridian.
   d. equator.

6. The distance between crests is the
   a. trough.
   b. wavelength.
   c. wave height.
   d. density.

7. Nodules are mostly nickel, iron, and
   a. manganese.
   b. chlorine.
   c. sodium.
   d. volcanic dust.

8. The process by which a gas changes to a liquid is called
   a. precipitation.
   b. evaporation.
   c. sublimation.
   d. condensation.

9. Just beyond the shoreline of a continent you would find a
   a. continental slope.
   b. continental shelf.
   c. deep sea trench.
   d. guyot.

10. Salinity of ocean water can rise when
    a. glaciers melt.
    b. it rains.
    c. water evaporates.
    d. runoff from rivers increases.

FILL IN **Write the term or phrase that best completes each sentence.**

11. Most of the water on Earth's surface is _____ water.

12. Oceanographers are specialists who study the _____.

13. Underwater research vessels are called _____.

14. Heat from the _____ warms ocean water.

15. Tides are caused mainly by the _____.

16. The time of low water level is _____ tide.

17. A ring-shaped coral reef around a lagoon is called an _____.

18. A guyot is an underwater, flat-topped _____.

Concept Challenges TEST PREP

WRITTEN RESPONSE **Answer each of the following questions in complete sentences.**

1. **CALCULATE:** If a sonar signal sent from a ship returns 8 seconds later, how deep is the ocean floor in that spot?

2. **EXPLAIN:** Why was a bathysphere considered an advancement in ocean exploration technology?

3. **PREDICT:** How would the salinity of the oceans be affected if increased temperatures caused the polar ice caps to melt into the oceans?

4. **COMPARE:** How can you tell the difference between a barrier reef and a fringing reef?

5. **DESCRIBE:** What are some specialties within the field of oceanography?

6. **COMPARE/CONTRAST:** How are oceans and seas alike and different?

7. **DESCRIBE:** What is the purpose of deep-sea drilling?

8. **ANALYZE:** What kinds of weathering and erosion change the shoreline?

INTERPRETING VISUALS **Use Figure 2-32 below to answer the following questions.**

9. How do you think the seafloor feature labeled *C* got its name?

10. What is the name of the landform labeled *D*?

11. How would the size of the shoreline change if sea levels rose due to global warming?

12. What parts of the continent, labeled *B*, *C*, and *G* on the diagram, extend into the ocean?

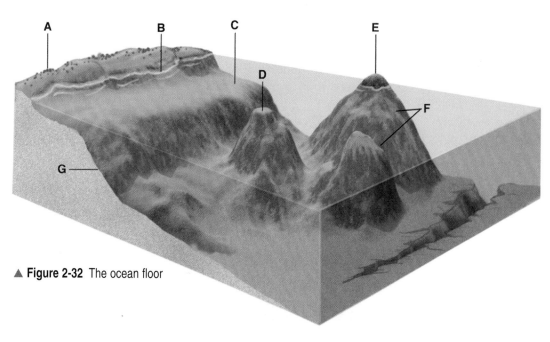

▲ **Figure 2-32** The ocean floor

Chapter 3 Air

▲ **Figure 3-1** Colorful balloons dot the sky as they gracefully rise in the atmosphere.

Heating air causes it to rise. This is how the balloons in the picture can rise and float. The heating and rising of air is how air currents are formed. Air currents affect the water cycle and weather patterns. Air thins out the higher you go in the atmosphere. Therefore, hot-air balloons cannot go too high.

▶What do you think would happen if you tried to take a balloon where there is very little air?

Contents

3-1 What is air?

Objectives
Describe air as matter. Identify and describe the main gases in air.

Key Terms
matter: anything that has mass and volume

atmosphere (AT-mohs-feer): envelope of gases that surrounds Earth

cellular respiration (rehs-puh-RAY-shuhn): process by which a cell releases energy from food molecules

A Mixture of Gases Air is a colorless, tasteless, odorless mixture of gases. Air is matter. **Matter** is anything that has mass and takes up space, or has volume.

◀ Figure 3-2
Air has mass and volume.

The **atmosphere,** or air, is the envelope of gases that surrounds Earth. Air is made up mostly of nitrogen and oxygen. Air is also made up of other gases. Figure 3-3 shows the approximate percentages of the gases that make up air.

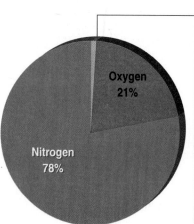

SOME OTHER GASES	
Gases	Percentage by Volume
Argon	0.934
Carbon dioxide	0.036
Neon	0.0018
Helium	0.00052
Hydrogen	0.00005
Krypton	0.00011
Methane	0.00002

▲ Figure 3-3 Gases in the air

 ANALYZE: What percentage of air is made up of helium, neon, and krypton?

Nitrogen About 78 percent of the atmosphere is nitrogen. All organisms need nitrogen. However, most living things cannot use nitrogen gas from the air.

Bacteria are microscopic organisms that live in soil, in water, and in the air. Some bacteria can change the nitrogen gas in the air into nitrogen compounds. Plants get the nitrogen they need by absorbing the nitrogen compounds made by these bacteria. Animals get the nitrogen they need by eating plants.

2 **DEFINE:** What are bacteria?

Oxygen About 21 percent of air is oxygen. Living things need oxygen to carry on cellular respiration. **Cellular respiration** is the process by which a cell releases energy from food molecules. The energy comes from the food made, eaten, or absorbed by an organism. Plants make their own food. Most animals must eat food. Some other organisms absorb food from their environment. Most living things get the oxygen they need from air.

 INFER: How do people get the oxygen they need to carry on respiration?

Carbon Dioxide About 0.04 percent of air is made up of carbon dioxide. Carbon dioxide is released when things burn. Respiration produces carbon dioxide as a byproduct. You get rid of this carbon dioxide when you breathe out. Plants need carbon dioxide to make their own food.

 STATE: How does carbon dioxide get into air?

Other Components in Air Most of the time, air looks and feels dry to us. However, it is never really completely dry. In addition to the gases mentioned above, air contains water vapor. Water vapor is water in the form of a gas. Steam is heated water vapor. Sometimes steam contains tiny droplets of water, which is what you see. The water vapor itself is invisible. The amount of water vapor in the air varies greatly from place to place and over time. In rain forests, up to 5 percent of the air may be water vapor.

Water vapor plays an important role in weather. Clouds form as water vapor condenses out of air that has cooled. It forms tiny drops of liquid water or crystals of ice. If these drops or crystals grow large enough, they can fall as rain or snow.

In addition to the gases that make it up, air contains tiny particles of dust, smoke, salt, and other chemicals. You can see some of these particles. They are not part of the air itself. They float in the air, and sometimes they make the air unhealthy to breathe.

 LIST: What is in air besides the gases?

CHECKING CONCEPTS

1. What two main gases make up air?
2. What is matter?
3. Why do living things need oxygen?
4. How does water vapor affect the weather?
5. What are two nongaseous particles in air?

THINKING CRITICALLY

6. **CONTRAST:** How is water vapor different from other gases that make up air?

INTERPRETING VISUALS

Use Figure 3-3 to answer the following questions.

7. **ESTIMATE:** What gas makes up most of air?
8. **CALCULATE:** What percentage of air is made up of methane, krypton, and hydrogen?
9. **IDENTIFY:** What gases make up the 1 percent of air not composed of nitrogen and oxygen?

Real-Life Science

BRONCHIAL ASTHMA

We all need air to live. For people who suffer from bronchial asthma, getting that air into their lungs can be a struggle. There are more than 14 million asthma sufferers in the United States alone.

An asthma attack usually starts with a swelling in the passages that carry air into our lungs when we breathe. One of the most common signs of an asthma attack is wheezing. Wheezing is the high-pitched noise caused by air moving through a narrowed air passage.

What causes an asthma attack? Usually, the air passages become irritated by tiny particles floating in the air. Often, these particles are things that a person with asthma is allergic to, such as pollen or animal fur. Household cleaners and cigarette smoke can also cause asthma attacks. The body's immune system releases a substance called histamine to fight the "invaders." It is the histamine that causes the swelling.

Asthma cannot be cured. Its symptoms can be controlled, though, with treatment.

Thinking Critically How can the condition of asthma be triggered by particles suspended in air?

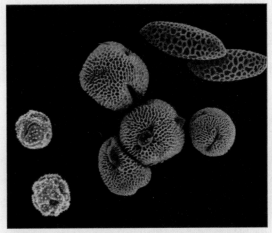
▲ **Figure 3-4** Three types of pollen grains

3-2 What are the layers of the atmosphere?

Objective
Name and describe the layers of the atmosphere.

Key Terms
troposphere (TROH-puh-sfeer)**:** lowest layer of the atmosphere

stratosphere (STRAT-uh-sfeer)**:** second layer of the atmosphere

mesosphere (MEHZ-uh-sfeer)**:** third layer of the atmosphere

thermosphere (THER-muh-sfeer)**:** upper layer of the atmosphere

Parts of the Atmosphere   The atmosphere begins at Earth's surface and goes more than 700 km up. Not all parts of the atmosphere are the same. The atmosphere is made up of four main layers. These layers are the troposphere, the stratosphere, the mesosphere, and the thermosphere.

▶ **1** LIST: What are the four main layers of the atmosphere?

The Troposphere   The **troposphere** is the layer of the atmosphere closest to Earth. The air you breathe into your lungs is part of the troposphere. Most of the water vapor found in the atmosphere is in the troposphere. This water vapor forms clouds. Weather takes place in the troposphere.

The higher you go in the troposphere, the colder it gets. Near the top of the troposphere, the temperature stops getting colder. The boundary between the troposphere and the layer above is called the tropopause.

▶ **2** DEFINE: What is the tropopause?

The Stratosphere   The stratosphere is the second layer of the atmosphere. The temperature of the air remains almost constant here. There is no weather in the stratosphere. Airplanes travel in this layer.

The upper stratosphere contains a layer of ozone. Ozone is a form of oxygen. Ozone prevents most of the ultraviolet light given off by the Sun from reaching Earth. Large amounts of ozone, however, are harmful to breathe and can irritate the lungs.

▶ **3** PREDICT: What might happen if the ozone layer of the stratosphere were destroyed?

The Mesosphere and Thermosphere   Above the stratosphere is the third layer of the atmosphere, the **mesosphere,** which means "middle layer." In the mesosphere, temperatures begin to fall again. Above the mesosphere is the fourth region, the **thermosphere.** Here temperatures actually rise with height. Beyond the thermosphere is mostly empty space. This region is called the exosphere.

From the mesosphere up to the top of the thermosphere is a broad region of space that contains many charged particles called ions. Radio waves sent from Earth are reflected or bounced off of these ions. Because of ions, radio signals can be sent between distant parts of Earth. The area where the ions are most concentrated is called the ionosphere.

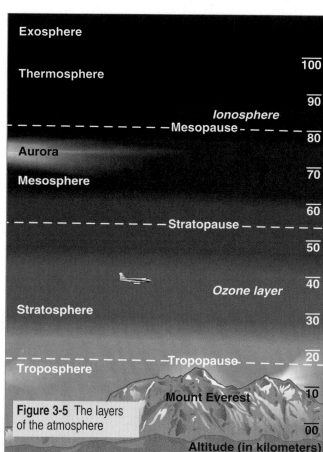

Figure 3-5 The layers of the atmosphere

Sometimes, in the night sky near the poles, you can see glowing colored light, usually green. These glowing lights, called auroras, are caused by charged particles from the Sun. The particles are interacting with matter in Earth's upper atmosphere. In the northern polar region, these events are known as the aurora borealis, or the northern lights. In the Southern Hemisphere, they are known as aurora australis.

▲ **Figure 3-6** The aurora borealis lights up the northern sky at night.

 DESCRIBE: How is the ionosphere used in communications?

 CHECKING CONCEPTS

1. The atmosphere is made up of _____ main layers.

2. The upper boundary of the troposphere is the _____.

3. Ozone is a form of _____.

THINKING CRITICALLY

4. **INFER:** Why do most airplanes travel in the stratosphere?

5. **COMPARE:** How do air temperatures differ in the troposphere and stratosphere?

INTERPRETING VISUALS

Use Figure 3-5 to answer the following questions.

6. **INFER:** In which layer of the atmosphere do we fly kites? Why?

7. **CALCULATE:** About how thick is the stratosphere?

8. **CALCULATE:** About how thick is the troposphere?

 Integrating Physical Science

TOPICS: air pressure, force

GETTING A LIFT INTO THE AIR

Daniel Bernoulli (bur-NOO-lee) was a Swiss scientist known for his work with fluids. Bernoulli found that the faster a fluid moves, the less pressure it exerts. Pressure is the amount of force acting on a surface. Bernoulli further stated that the pressure of a moving stream of fluid or gas is lower than the pressure of any fluid or gas around it. This explains how air moving around a wing can produce a force called lift, allowing an airplane to fly.

Objects can be designed so that air moves at different speeds around them. If the air moves faster above the object, pressure pushes the object upward.

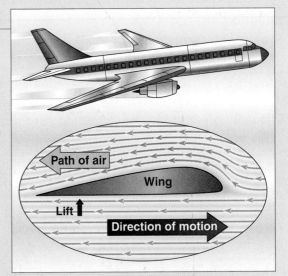

▲ **Figure 3-7** Airplane wings are curved on top, like bird wings.

Like a bird's wing, the top of an airplane wing is curved. Air that moves over the top of the wing must travel farther than air that moves along the bottom. The air moving over the top moves faster so its pressure is lower than the air pressure on the bottom. This difference in pressure creates the lift.

Thinking Critically Why are airplane wings curved on top?

INVESTIGATE

Modeling the Absorption of Light
HANDS-ON ACTIVITY

1. Place an aluminum plate under a lamp whose light is directed downward.

2. Fill half the plate with dry, dark soil and half with dry sand.

3. Insert a thermometer into each side. Record the temperatures.

4. Turn on the lamp and let the plate stand for a while. Compare the new temperatures with the starting ones.

THINK ABOUT IT: How do the temperatures change? Why is one higher than the other?

STEP 4

Objective

Describe how energy from the Sun warms Earth's surface.

Key Terms

radiant (RAY-dee-uhnt) **energy:** energy given off by the Sun that can travel through empty space

radiation (ray-dee-AY-shuhn)**:** movement of the Sun's energy through empty space

Radiant Energy The Sun gives off **radiant energy.** If you go out into the sunlight, you can feel the radiant energy from the Sun warming your skin.

Light is a form of radiant energy. Radiant energy can travel across millions of kilometers of empty space. The movement of this energy through empty space is called **radiation.** Most of Earth's energy comes from the radiation given off by the Sun.

1 **NAME:** What kind of energy is sunlight?

Absorption of Energy Dark surfaces absorb light. When light is absorbed, or taken in, it is usually changed into heat.

Suppose you wrap two ice cubes with cloth. You wrap one ice cube in a dark-colored cloth and the other in light-colored cloth. You place both ice cubes in sunlight. Which one would melt first?

100% Sun's energy

20% absorbed by gases, clouds, and dust

30% reflected by clouds, dust, air, and Earth's surface

Dust particles

Figure 3-8 Radiant energy is absorbed or reflected, depending on what it comes into contact with in the atmosphere.

50% absorbed by Earth's surface

The ice cube wrapped in the dark cloth would melt faster. Surfaces that reflect light, such as white surfaces, remain cooler than surfaces that absorb light, such as dark surfaces.

 DESCRIBE: What happens when light is absorbed by a surface?

Energy from the Sun Only a small part of the Sun's energy reaches Earth. Some of the Sun's energy is absorbed by the atmosphere. Clouds, dust particles, and water droplets in the atmosphere also absorb or reflect some of the Sun's energy. The energy that is reflected goes back into space. Some of the energy that passes through the atmosphere is absorbed by Earth's surface. This energy is changed into heat. As a result, Earth becomes warmer. The entire process is shown in Figure 3-10.

 STATE: What happens when the Sun's energy is absorbed by Earth's surface?

✓ CHECKING CONCEPTS

1. Light is a type of _____.
2. The Sun's energy reaches Earth by _____.

3. When light is _____, it is changed into heat.
4. Clouds, _____, and water droplets can absorb or reflect the Sun's energy.

 ## THINKING CRITICALLY

5. **PREDICT:** If there was no wind, would it be cooler on a cloudy or on a clear day? Why?

Web InfoSearch

Electromagnetic Radiation Electromagnetic radiation is energy in the form of waves of different frequencies. Frequency refers to how often the wave occurs in a given amount of time. Light is only one type of electromagnetic radiation.

SEARCH: Use the Internet to find out more about this. What are other types of electromagnetic radiation? In what technologies are they used? Start your search at www.conceptsandchallenges.com. Some key search words are **electromagnetic radiation, light waves,** and **X-rays.**

 ## Science and Technology
SOLAR ENERGY

The Sun is a potentially huge source of energy. It could be used to meet all of the world's energy needs. Scientists are working to develop efficient ways to use solar energy.

At one power plant in California's Mohave Desert, rings of huge mirrors capture sunlight and reflect it to a central tower. A liquid runs through pipes in the tower. The liquid becomes hot. The hot liquid is then used to boil water to make steam. The steam turns a turbine and a generator. In this way, solar energy can be converted to produce electricity when people need it, even after sunset.

▲ Figure 3-9 On this artist's drawing of a communications satellite, the large blue panels contain the solar cells.

Solar cells can also be used to turn solar energy directly into electricity. Solar cells are also called photovoltaic, or PV, cells. In the 1950s, PV cells were developed for use on U.S. spacecraft. Panels of solar cells power satellites in space. You might have a calculator or a watch that uses a solar cell. Some small, experimental cars are powered by solar cells.

Thinking Critically Why is it important to develop solar energy for heating homes?

3-4 How does heat move through the atmosphere?

Objective
Explain how the atmosphere is heated.

Key Terms
conduction (kuhn-DUK-shuhn): transfer of heat through matter by direct contact

convection (kuhn-VEK-shuhn): process by which heat is transferred through a liquid or a gas

Conduction Heat moves through Earth's atmosphere in three main ways. These ways are conduction, radiation, and convection.

The troposphere, or lower layer of the atmosphere, is heated by a process that moves heat through matter. A metal pan placed over a flame will get hot. The metal molecules directly over the flame begin to move faster. They bump into the slower-moving molecules surrounding them and make them move faster. This is how heat moves through the metal pan.

Heat generally moves from an area of higher temperature to an area of lower temperature. This kind of movement of heat through matter is called **conduction.**

Sunlight absorbed by Earth's surface is changed into heat. This warms the surface. Air touches the warmed surface and is heated by conduction.

1 NAME: How does heat move through matter?

Radiation The atmosphere is also heated by the process of radiation. Radiant energy travels from the Sun through space in waves.

Most of the Sun's energy is short-wave radiation. This radiation passes easily through the atmosphere and strikes Earth's surface, where it is mostly absorbed and changed into heat energy. Heat energy is long-wave radiation. Earth's surface warms up and radiates most of the heat energy back into the atmosphere. There it is absorbed by gases. This warms the atmosphere.

2 DESCRIBE: What happens to the energy radiated by Earth?

Convection The process by which heat is transferred through a gas or a liquid is called **convection.** When air is heated, it expands. As the warm air expands, it becomes lighter because it becomes less dense. Warm air is lighter than cool air. Warm air rises. The cooler, denser air sinks.

3 DEFINE: What is convection?

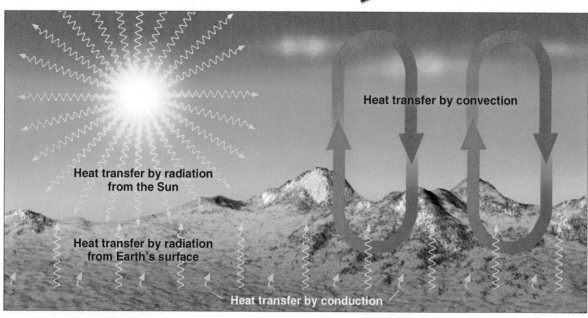

Heat transfer by convection

Heat transfer by radiation from the Sun

Heat transfer by radiation from Earth's surface

Heat transfer by conduction

◄ Figure 3-10
There are three types of heat transfer: conduction, radiation, and convection.

✓ CHECKING CONCEPTS

1. When a solid is heated, its _____ move faster.
2. Solids are heated by _____ .
3. Earth's radiant energy is _____ -wave radiation.
4. Energy traveling in waves from the Sun is called _____ energy.
5. Heat moves through air by _____ .

THINKING CRITICALLY

6. **IDENTIFY:** Which of the following is conduction, which is radiation, and which is convection?
   a. The water in a fish tank becomes warmer after the heater in it is turned on.
   b. The Sun warms your skin on a summer day.
   c. A glass bowl is warmed by the steaming rice it contains.
   d. A burning log in a fireplace causes the temperature in a room to go up.

INTERPRETING VISUALS

Use Figure 3-11 to answer the following questions.

7. **EXPLAIN:** Why does the balloon rise?
8. **INFER:** What does the flame do?

▲ **Figure 3-11** Hot-air balloons

HEALTH AND SAFETY TIP

Never grab the handle of a hot pot with your bare hands. Use a potholder. Metal is a good conductor of heat. The potholder is not. It keeps most of the heat from passing through to your hands.

Hands-On Activity

DETERMINING THE EFFECT OF TEMPERATURE ON AIR MOVEMENT

You will need scissors, a ruler, tissue paper, thread, cellophane tape, a desk lamp, and a partner.

1. Cut a 6-cm long spiral from the tissue paper.
2. Cut a piece of thread 15 cm long.
3. Tape one end of the thread to the center of the paper spiral.
4. Turn on the desk lamp. Point the light up.
5. Have your partner hold the end of the thread. Position the paper spiral about 10 cm above the light. ⚠ CAUTION: Do not allow the paper to touch the light bulb.

▲ **STEP 5** Be sure the spiral does not touch the light bulb.

Practicing Your Skills

6. **DESCRIBE:** What happens to the spiral?
7. **INFER:** How do temperature differences affect what happens?
8. **CONCLUDE:** How is this an example of convection?

3-5 What is air pressure?

INVESTIGATE

Observing Air Pressure
HANDS-ON ACTIVITY

1. Place a drinking straw in a cup of water.

2. Put your finger over the top end of the straw.

3. Take the straw out of the water. Observe the water inside the straw.

4. Hold the straw over the cup and remove your finger. Observe what happens.

THINK ABOUT IT: What happened when you removed the straw from the water with your finger on top of it? What holds the water in the straw? Why does the water fall out when you take your finger away? How is this activity related to air pressure?

STEP 3

Objective

Explain air pressure and describe what affects it.

Key Terms

newton: metric unit of force

pressure: amount of force per unit of area

Weight and Pressure Weight is a force. If you hold a book in the palm of your hand, you feel the weight of the book pressing down. This force is measured in units called **newtons (N).** A 1-kg mass has a force of about 10 N.

The amount of force per unit of area is called **pressure.** When you hold the book in the palm of your hand, the book's weight is spread over your hand. Suppose the book's force is 10 N, and your hand has an area of 100 square cm, or 100 cm². The force on each square centimeter is then 10 N divided by 100 cm², or 0.1 N/cm². The pressure of the book on your hand is 0.1 N/cm².

$$\frac{\text{Force}}{\text{Area}} = \text{Pressure}$$

$$\frac{10\ \text{N}}{100\ \text{cm}^2} = 0.1\ \text{N/cm}^2$$

A force exerted over a small area causes more pressure than the same force applied over a large area. See Figure 3-12 for an example of this.

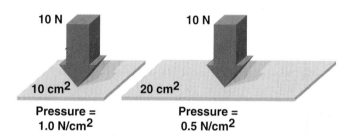
10 N   10 N

10 cm²   20 cm²

Pressure = 1.0 N/cm²   **Pressure = 0.5 N/cm²**

▲ **Figure 3-12** The same force exerted over a smaller area causes more pressure.

Air has weight. One liter of air weighs about 0.01 N at sea level. This is about the weight of a paper clip. The surface of Earth is at the bottom of the atmosphere. Air molecules are in constant motion and are pulled towards Earth's center by gravity. The force of all these moving molecules causes air pressure. Most of the air in the atmosphere is concentrated near Earth's surface. So air pressure is greatest near Earth's surface and decreases as altitude increases.

▶ **EXPLAIN:** Why does air exert pressure on Earth's surface?

Elevation Air pressure changes with elevation, or height above sea level. The atmosphere is hundreds of kilometers thick. The weight of all this air causes more pressure near the ground. This pushes the air molecules closer together. Near the top of the atmosphere, the air molecules remain farther apart. There is very little weight of air pressing down. Therefore, the air pressure is lower. The higher the elevation, the lower the air pressure.

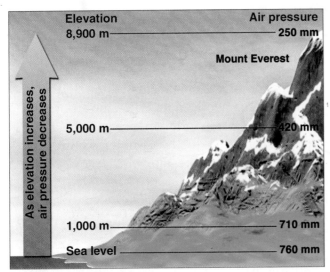

▲ **Figure 3-13** Elevation affects air pressure, which is measured in millimeters of mercury.

Air pressure decreases as distance above the surface increases. The air pressure on top of a mountain is less than the air pressure at sea level. Air pressure at sea level is about 10 N/cm².

2 ▶ **DESCRIBE:** How does elevation affect air pressure?

Water Vapor The more water vapor in the air, the lower the air pressure. Water evaporates from lakes, rivers, and oceans. Living things give off water vapor. All of this water vapor goes into the air. The lighter molecules of water vapor replace some of the other gas molecules in air. Air with a lot of water vapor weighs less than dry air with less water vapor. Thus, moist air exerts less pressure. Air pressure goes down as the amount of water vapor in the air goes up.

▲ **Figure 3-14** The weather conditions outside influence the air pressure.

3 ▶ **DESCRIBE:** How does water vapor affect air pressure?

Temperature Under ordinary conditions, the higher the temperature, the lower the air pressure. Heat makes air molecules move faster. As the molecules move faster, they spread apart. This makes the air less dense.

So warm air is less dense than cool air. In summer, when temperatures are higher, the air pressure is usually lower.

4 ▶ **RELATE:** How is temperature related to air pressure?

✔ CHECKING CONCEPTS

1. Pressure is the amount of _____ on a unit of area.
2. Air pressure at sea level is _____ than air pressure on top of a mountain.
3. Air pressure _____ as elevation increases.
4. Warm air weighs _____ than cool air.

💡 THINKING CRITICALLY

5. **CALCULATE:** A 5-N force pushes down on an area that is 10 cm². How much pressure does the force have?
6. **HYPOTHESIZE:** Why do ears "pop" in an airplane?

Web InfoSearch

The Magdeburg Hemispheres In 1654, Otto von Guericke, the mayor of a small German town called Magdeburg, did an experiment. He made a hollow metal sphere with two halves, or hemispheres, fitted tightly together. Air was pumped out of the sphere through a valve. This lowered the air pressure inside. The higher outside air pressure held the sphere together.

SEARCH: Use the Internet to find out more about this experiment. Why couldn't horses pull the two hemispheres apart? Start your search at www.conceptsandchallenges.com. Some key search words are **air pressure, Von Guericke,** and **Magdeburg.**

How is air pressure measured?

Objective

Explain how a barometer measures air pressure.

Key Term

barometer (buh-RAHM-uht-uhr)**:** instrument used to measure air pressure

Mercury Barometer Air pressure is measured with an instrument called a **barometer.** A mercury barometer is a glass tube filled with mercury. It is open at one end. The space at the closed end of the tube forms a vacuum. The open end of the tube sits in a container of mercury. Air pressure pushes down on the surface of the mercury in the container. The mercury is pushed up the vacuum. At sea level, air pressure can raise a column of mercury to a height of 760 mm. As the air pressure changes, the level of mercury in the tube rises or falls.

▲ Figure 3-15 Near the ocean, a mercury barometer (on right) shows a reading of 760 mm.

▶ **1 DEFINE:** What does a barometer do?

Aneroid Barometer Another kind of barometer is called an aneroid barometer. The word *aneroid* means "without liquid." An aneroid barometer is made of an airtight metal container. The sides of the container are very thin. They can bend in or out.

When the air pressure increases, the sides of the metal container bend in. When the air pressure decreases, the sides of the container bend out. A pointer is connected to the container. As the container changes shape, the pointer moves along a scale. The scale shows air pressure in millimeters of mercury. Some aneroid barometers, called barographs, keep a continuous record of air pressure.

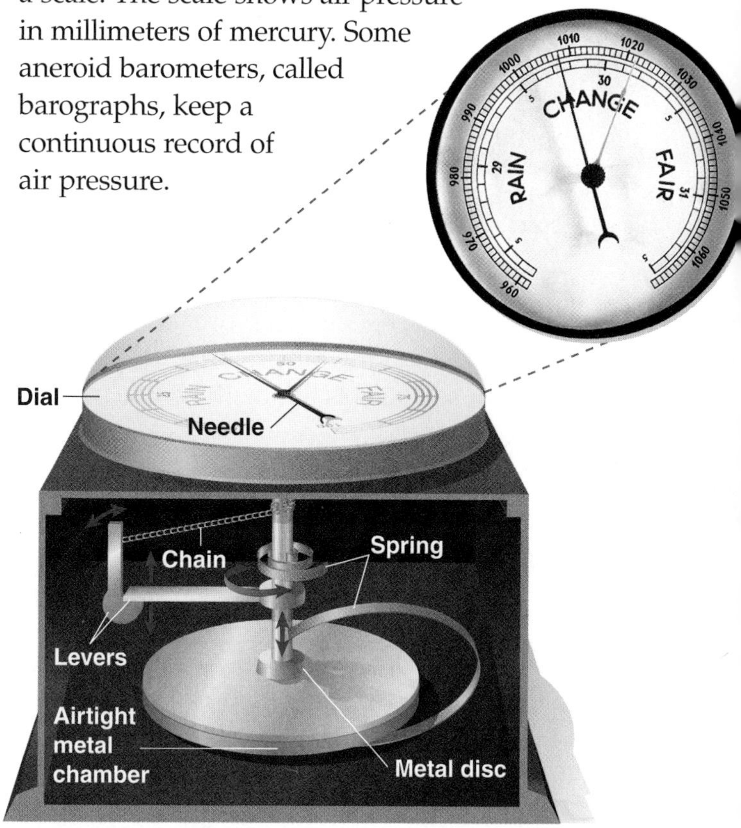

Dial — Needle — Chain — Spring — Levers — Airtight metal chamber — Metal disc

▲ Figure 3-16 Aneroid barometer

▶ **2 DESCRIBE:** How does an aneroid barometer work?

Measuring Air Pressure Standard air pressure at sea level measures 760 mm of mercury. This is sometimes called one atmosphere. Air pressure is also measured in millibars (mb). Standard air pressure is equal to 1,013.20 mb.

▶ **3 ANALYZE:** How many millimeters of mercury equal 1,013.20 mb?

Measuring Altitude An altimeter is a device used to measure altitude. Pilots, scientists, surveyors, and mountain climbers all use altimeters.

At sea level, air pressure will raise a column of mercury 760 mm. As you go higher, air pressure decreases. The mercury column drops.

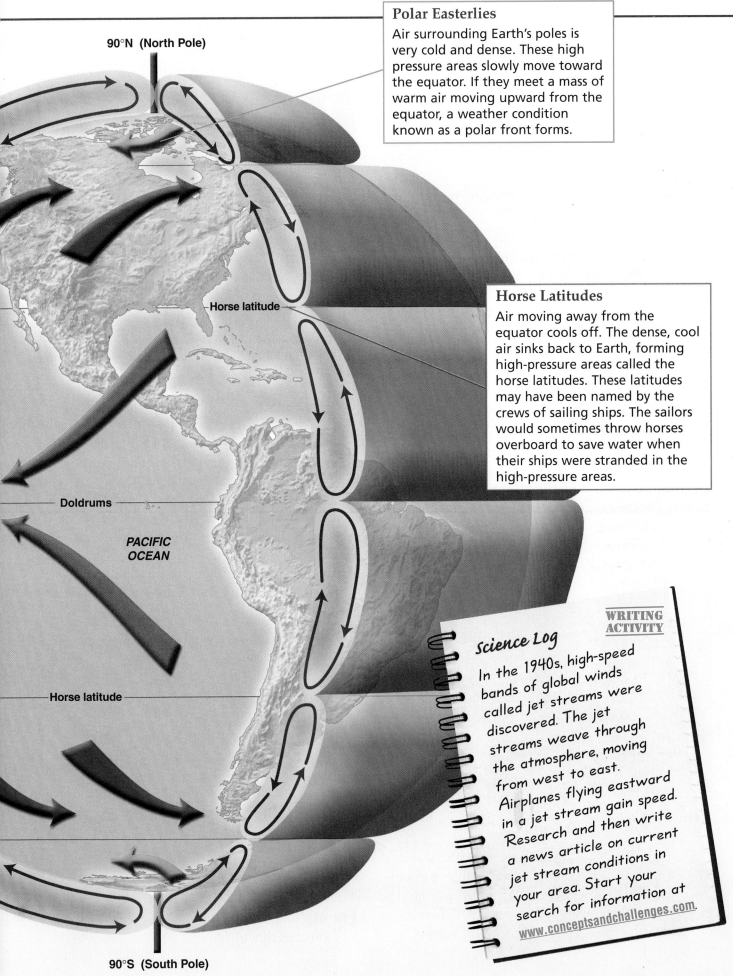

90°N (North Pole)

Polar Easterlies

Air surrounding Earth's poles is very cold and dense. These high pressure areas slowly move toward the equator. If they meet a mass of warm air moving upward from the equator, a weather condition known as a polar front forms.

Horse latitude

Horse Latitudes

Air moving away from the equator cools off. The dense, cool air sinks back to Earth, forming high-pressure areas called the horse latitudes. These latitudes may have been named by the crews of sailing ships. The sailors would sometimes throw horses overboard to save water when their ships were stranded in the high-pressure areas.

Doldrums

PACIFIC OCEAN

Horse latitude

WRITING ACTIVITY

Science Log

In the 1940s, high-speed bands of global winds called jet streams were discovered. The jet streams weave through the atmosphere, moving from west to east. Airplanes flying eastward in a jet stream gain speed. Research and then write a news article on current jet stream conditions in your area. Start your search for information at www.conceptsandchallenges.com.

90°S (South Pole)

3-8 What causes local winds?

Objective
Describe patterns of local winds.

Key Term
monsoon: wind that changes direction with the seasons

Sea and Land Breezes All winds are produced by temperature differences caused by unequal heating of Earth's surface. Local winds are simply small-scale winds produced by local changes in air pressure.

A breeze coming from the sea toward the land is a sea breeze. A breeze going from the land toward the sea is a land breeze. Land and sea breezes are local winds.

The Sun heats land faster than it does water. As a result, air over the land is warmer and lighter than air over the water. The cooler, heavier air over the ocean moves in toward the land. The warmer, lighter air over the land rises. The result is a sea breeze.

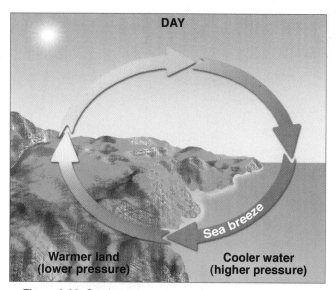

▲ **Figure 3-23** Sea breeze

At night, the land cools faster than the water. The air over the land becomes cooler than the air over the water. The heavier air over the land moves toward the water. The warmer, lighter air over the water rises. The result is a land breeze.

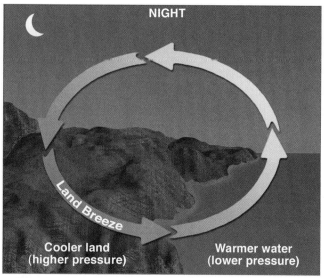

▲ **Figure 3-24** Land breeze

▶ **1** COMPARE: Which cools faster, land or water?

Mountain and Valley Breezes Mountain regions also have local winds. During the day, the air on a mountain slope is warmer than the air in the valleys. Warm air has low pressure. Air in the valley is cooler and has high pressure. Air moves from the high pressure of the valley to the low pressure of the mountain slope. This is a valley breeze. At night, the valleys are warmer than the mountaintops. The heavier mountain air moves downhill toward the valley. This is a mountain breeze.

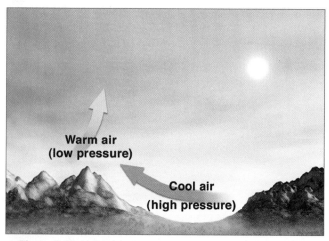

▲ **Figure 3-25** Valley breeze

▶ **2** DESCRIBE: In which direction do valley breezes move?

Monsoons Parts of some continents have winds that change direction with the seasons. These winds are called **monsoons.**

In the summer, when the land is warmer than the water, winds move from the ocean toward the land. In the winter, when the land is colder than the water, the winds move from the land toward the ocean. Winds blow toward the ocean all winter. India is famous for its monsoons. The summer monsoon brings warm, moist air with heavy rains. The winter monsoon carries dry air. There is little rain in winter.

 DEFINE: What are monsoons?

✓ CHECKING CONCEPTS

1. A sea breeze blows toward the _____ from the ocean.

2. Land is heated _____ than water.

3. Movement of air from the land toward the ocean is called a _____ breeze.

4. A _____ breeze moves downhill toward a valley.

5. Winds that change direction with the seasons are _____.

 THINKING CRITICALLY

6. **ANALYZE:** During part of the year, monsoons bring heavy rains and warm temperatures to many countries. Do these rainy seasons occur in the summer or winter? Explain.

7. **MODEL:** Draw and label a diagram of a mountain breeze. Use Figure 3-25 to help you.

BUILDING READING SKILLS

Vocabulary Mistral, foehn (FAYN), and chinook are the names of three local winds. Use a dictionary or other references to look up each of these winds. Write a brief description of each wind on a sheet of paper. Where does each wind occur?

 ## Science and Technology

WIND ENERGY

For years, farmers have used windmills to pump water. Today, many communities are using the wind to produce electricity. Modern materials and engineering could combine to make wind energy an important source of power for the future. Wind energy is a promising source of power because the wind is free and no pollution is produced. However, the speed and direction of the winds are unpredictable.

In some places, large windmill farms provide power for electric generators. Windmill farms may include hundreds or even thousands of windmills. Over 6,000 wind generators located at Altamont Pass, east of San Francisco, California, are already in operation and producing electricity. One of the largest windmills is in Medicine Bow, Wyoming. This one windmill can provide enough electricity for 1,200 homes.

Modern windmills do not look much like the windmills used to pump water on farms. Some of the newer windmills look more like airplane propellers or eggbeaters. Instead of wood, they are made of new, lightweight materials.

Thinking Critically Why are fields with many windmills called wind farms?

▲ **Figure 3-26** A large windmill farm near Palm Springs, California

3-9 How is wind measured?

Objective
Explain how weather instruments are used to describe wind.

Key Terms
wind vane: instrument that indicates wind direction

anemometer (an-uh-MAHM-uht-uhr): instrument that measures wind speed

Showing Wind Direction Both wind speed and wind direction are significant to weather watchers. A wind is named for the direction from which it comes. If a wind comes from the north, it is a north wind. If it comes from the east, it is an east wind.

The direction of a wind is determined with a wind vane. A **wind vane** shows the direction a wind is coming from. Many wind vanes are shaped like arrows. When the wind blows, the arrow turns and points into the wind. Often the direction of the wind is shown on a dial connected to the wind vane. The dial may indicate wind direction by points on a compass (E, W, N, S) or by degrees on a scale.

▲ **Figure 3-27** A wind vane indicates wind direction.

▶ **NAME:** What is a wind that blows from the northeast named?

Measuring Wind Speed An **anemometer** is an instrument used to measure wind speed. It is often made of cups turned on their sides. These cups are attached to rods. Wind blowing against the cups causes the anemometer to turn. The faster and stronger the wind, the faster the anemometer turns. Anemometers usually have a meter attached to them that measures how fast the wind is blowing. It does this by measuring how fast the cups turn.

▲ **Figure 3-28** An anemometer measures wind speed.

▶ **DESCRIBE:** How does an anemometer work?

Weather Balloons Scientists sometimes use weather balloons to determine wind speed and direction. A weather balloon is filled with the gas helium. Helium gas is lighter than air. As a result, balloons filled with helium gas rise into the air.

▲ **Figure 3-29** Weather balloons often carry instrument packages called radiosondes. These contain temperature, pressure, and humidity sensors.

Winds high in the troposphere move a weather balloon along. Scientists can measure the speed of the wind by measuring the speed at which the balloon moves along. The direction it moves shows wind direction.

3 IDENTIFY: What do weather balloons measure?

✔ CHECKING CONCEPTS

1. Winds are named based upon the _____ from which they come.
2. Wind direction is shown with a _____ .
3. Wind speed is measured with an _____.
4. Weather balloons are filled with _____.
5. Helium gas is _____ than air.

THINKING CRITICALLY

6. **INFER:** A weather vane points to the north. From which direction is the wind blowing?
7. **HYPOTHESIZE:** If carbon dioxide is heavier than air, can it be used in a weather balloon? Explain.

8. **INFER:** Why is it important for weather forecasters to know the speed and direction of the wind?
9. **INFER:** What happens to the cups on an anemometer when the wind gusts?

BUILDING SCIENCE SKILLS

Classifying Winds are classified by their speed or strength. They are also classified by the damage they do to homes and property. Place each wind below in order from calmest to strongest.

a. Hurricane: great damage is done to buildings
b. Strong breeze: hard to walk against the wind and open umbrellas
c. Calm: smoke goes straight up
d. Gale: branches are broken from trees; store windows break; TV antennas break
e. Moderate to fresh breeze: small trees sway; papers are blown around
f. Strong gale: trees are uprooted

Hands-On Activity

MAKING A WIND VANE

You will need cardboard, glue, a ballpoint pen cover, a compass, a pencil, and scissors.

1. Cut out two cardboard arrows about the same size.
   ⚠ CAUTION: Be careful when using scissors.
2. Clip a ballpoint pen cover in the middle between the two arrows. Then, glue the two arrows together.
3. Place the pen cover on the point of a pencil. Move the cover back and forth between the arrows until the arrow balances.
4. Go outside and hold up your vane where the wind will not be blocked by buildings or trees. Use a compass to see where the arrow points.

▲ **STEP 4** Hold your wind vane where the wind can blow it freely.

Practicing Your Skills

5. **INFER:** In what direction does your wind vane point?
6. **ANALYZE:** A strong wind would blow your cardboard vane away. What could you use to make a more sturdy wind vane?

Chapter Summary

Lesson 3-1

- The **atmosphere** is an envelope of gases that surrounds Earth. About 78% of air is nitrogen, 21% is oxygen, and 0.04% is carbon dioxide.

Lesson 3-2

- The atmosphere is made up of four basic layers. The **troposphere** is the lowest layer. The **stratosphere** is the second layer. The ozone layer here protects us from harmful rays from the Sun. The third layer is the **mesosphere.** The fourth is the **thermosphere.** Within the mesosphere and thermosphere are concentrations of ions useful in radio communications.

Lessons 3-3 and 3-4

- The Sun gives off **radiant energy** that travels through space by **radiation.** When light energy is absorbed, it is changed into heat energy. Earth's surface changes light energy into heat energy.

- Heat moves through matter and the troposphere by **conduction.** It moves through the entire atmosphere by **convection.**

Lessons 3-5 and 3-6

- **Pressure** is the amount of force per unit of area. The weight of the air in the atmosphere exerts pressure on Earth's surface.

- Air pressure is affected by altitude, temperature, and water vapor.

- A **barometer** measures air pressure. Barometers can be mercury or aneroid.

- Air pressure is measured in millimeters of mercury or in millibars.

Lessons 3-7, 3-8, and 3-9

- **Air currents** are caused by the unequal heating of air. **Wind** is air moving horizontally along Earth's surface. Winds are caused by air pressure differences.

- Land breezes and sea breezes are local winds. Mountain regions have local winds called mountain breezes and valley breezes. A **monsoon** is a wind that changes direction with the seasons.

- A **wind vane** measures wind direction. An **anemometer** measures wind speed. Weather balloons measure wind speed and direction.

Key Term Challenges

air current (p. 74)
anemometer (p. 80)
atmosphere (p. 60)
barometer (p. 70)
cellular respiration (p. 60)
conduction (p. 66)
convection (p. 66)
matter (p. 60)
mesosphere (p. 62)
monsoon (p. 78)
newton (p. 68)
pressure (p. 68)
radiant energy (p. 64)
radiation (p. 64)
stratosphere (p. 62)
thermosphere (p. 62)
troposphere (p. 62)
wind (p. 74)
wind vane (p. 80)

MATCHING Write the Key Term from above that best matches each description.

1. anything with mass and volume
2. envelope of gases that surrounds Earth
3. process by which a cell releases energy from food molecules
4. upper layer of the atmosphere
5. movement of heat through matter
6. wind that changes direction with the seasons
7. lowest layer of the atmosphere
8. horizontal movement of air

IDENTIFYING WORD RELATIONSHIPS Explain how the words in each pair are related. Write your answers in complete sentences.

9. radiant energy, radiation
10. newton, pressure
11. wind, anemometer
12. convection, air current
13. breeze, local wind
14. wind, wind vane
15. stratosphere, troposphere

Content Challenges TEST PREP

MULTIPLE CHOICE Write the letter of the term or phrase that best completes each statement.

1. An altimeter measures
   a. wind speed.
   b. wind direction.
   c. altitude.
   d. rainfall.

2. Seventy-eight percent of the air is made up of
   a. nitrogen.
   b. oxygen.
   c. helium.
   d. carbon dioxide.

3. The layer of atmosphere closest to Earth is
   a. the tropopause.
   b. the stratosphere.
   c. the ionosphere.
   d. the troposphere.

4. The region of the atmosphere that reflects radio signals is the
   a. tropopause.
   b. stratosphere.
   c. ionosphere.
   d. troposphere.

5. Heat travels through empty space by
   a. convection.
   b. conduction.
   c. evaporation.
   d. radiation.

6. Earth's surface is heated by
   a. ozone.
   b. conduction.
   c. ions.
   d. radiation.

7. Air pressure is measured with
   a. a barometer.
   b. an altimeter.
   c. a wind vane.
   d. an anemometer.

8. Regions of cold, heavy air are called
   a. highs.
   b. lows.
   c. convections.
   d. monsoons.

9. A wind that blows from the southwest is a
   a. southwest wind.
   b. monsoon.
   c. local wind.
   d. northeast wind.

10. Sea breezes and land breezes are two kinds of
    a. local winds.
    b. monsoons.
    c. jet streams.
    d. global winds.

FILL IN Write the term or phrase that best completes each sentence.

11. Heat moves through _____ by conduction.

12. Heat moves through liquids and _____ by convection.

13. During respiration, living things give off _____ and water vapor as byproducts.

14. Air is a _____ of gases.

15. Oxygen, argon, and _____ are the three main gases in air.

16. Beyond the atmosphere is the region known as the _____.

17. The ozone layer of the stratosphere protects Earth from _____ light from the Sun.

18. Ozone is a form of _____.

19. When air is heated, it _____.

20. Cool air is heavier and more _____ than warm air.

Concept Challenges TEST PREP

WRITTEN RESPONSE Answer each of the following questions in complete sentences.

1. **ANALYZE:** As elevation increases, what happens to air pressure? Explain why it does this.

2. **EXPLAIN:** How does a wind vane indicate wind direction?

3. **PREDICT:** Would air pressure on top of a mountain be greater in the summer or in the winter? Explain.

4. **EXPLAIN:** Why do you think mercury is used in barometers instead of water?

5. **INFER:** How do mountain and valley breezes get their names?

6. **CONTRAST:** How is a wind vane different from an anemometer?

7. **HYPOTHESIZE:** Why would dark-colored clothing be warmer in the winter than light-colored clothing?

8. **INFER:** Why are most wind vanes shaped like arrows?

INTERPRETING VISUALS Use Figure 3-30 to answer the following questions.

9. What is shown in the diagram?

10. In what layer of the atmosphere do auroras occur?

11. What are the names of the layers of the atmosphere?

12. What is the name of the upper part of the atmosphere?

13. How far does the troposphere extend?

14. Where is the ozone layer located?

15. What is the name of the layer of the atmosphere in which most weather takes place?

16. What kinds of particles make up most of the upper atmosphere?

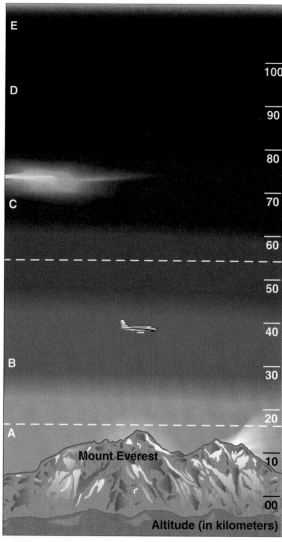

▲ Figure 3-30

Chapter 4 Weather

▲ **Figure 4-1** Severe thunderstorms produce lightning and sometimes even tornadoes.

Every day, about 40,000 thunderstorms occur around the world. Most of these develop in the regions near the equator. The power of a thunderstorm can be enormous. Bright bolts of lightning flash across the sky. This is followed by the ear-splitting roar of thunder. Many thunderstorms bring heavy rains or strong winds. Sometimes there is even hail or tornadoes.

▶What evidence of a storm is there in this picture?

Contents

Where does water in the atmosphere come from?

Objective
Explain how water gets into the atmosphere.

Key Terms
evaporation (ee-vap-uh-RAY-shuhn)**:** changing of a liquid to a gas

transpiration (tran-spuh-RAY-shuhn)**:** process by which plants give off water vapor into the air

Water Vapor

On a warm day, droplets of water may form on the outside of a window. The window surface is cooler than the outside air. The water comes from the air. Water in air is in the form of a gas called water vapor. Water vapor is an odorless,

▲ **Figure 4-2** Up to 5 percent of the water in the rain forests may be in the form of water vapor.

colorless gas. It mixes freely with other gases in the atmosphere. Most other gases change state only under extreme conditions. Water changes state at ordinary temperatures and pressures. It is because of these changes of state at ordinary temperatures that water leaves the oceans as a gas and returns again as a liquid. Water is also found in the atmosphere as clouds and fog. These are made up of tiny droplets of water or ice.

The amount of water vapor in the air varies from place to place and over time. However, it has been estimated that there are a total of about 14 million tons of water vapor in the atmosphere.

▶ **NAME:** What is water called when it is a gas?

Evaporation

Water vapor enters the air through the process of evaporation. **Evaporation** is the changing of a liquid to a gas. Most of the water in the air evaporates from the oceans.

Every day, millions of tons of water evaporate from the surface of the oceans. Water also evaporates from lakes, rivers, puddles, and wet soil. Winds carry the water vapor in the air all over Earth's surface.

▶ **IDENTIFY:** Where does most of the water in the air come from?

Heat and Evaporation

Molecules in a liquid are always moving. Some are moving faster than others. Some of the fast-moving molecules near the surface escape from the liquid. They enter and become part of the air. This is evaporation.

When a liquid is heated, its molecules move faster. More of the molecules can escape from the surface. Evaporation occurs more rapidly in warm liquids. Water in a pan over a heater evaporates faster than does water in a pan on a table. Evaporation from the oceans occurs most rapidly around the equator, where the water is heated by the more direct rays of the Sun.

▲ **Figure 4-3** Near the equator, evaporation occurs rapidly.

▶ **DESCRIBE:** What causes a liquid to evaporate faster?

Living Things and Water Vapor If you blow on a cold mirror, moisture forms on it. When it is cold outside, you can see your breath. This is water vapor changing back into liquid water droplets. Breathing adds moisture to air. Plants also give off water vapor through a process called **transpiration.** Transpiration occurs in the leaves of plants through tiny openings called stomata.

◄ **Figure 4-4**
Stomata, or tiny openings, on a leaf release water vapor.

 NAME: How do plants give off water vapor?

✔ CHECKING CONCEPTS

1. About how much water vapor is in the air?
2. How do animals add water to the air?

3. What happens to the molecules in a liquid when they are heated?
4. What part of a plant gives off water vapor through openings called stomata?
5. What is the gaseous form of water called?

THINKING CRITICALLY

6. **IDENTIFY:** Where does most of the moisture in the air come from?
7. **HYPOTHESIZE:** If you wipe a damp cloth across a tabletop, the table is wet. What will probably happen to the water in a few minutes? Why?

DESIGNING AN EXPERIMENT

Design an experiment to solve the following problem. Include a hypothesis, materials needed, variables, a procedure, and a type of data to study. Also tell how you would record your data.

PROBLEM: How can you show that heated water evaporates faster than unheated water?

 Hands-On Activity

OBSERVING TRANSPIRATION

You will need a small potted houseplant, a twist tie, a clear plastic bag, and a graduated cylinder.

1. Carefully cover the plant with the plastic bag. Use a twist tie to secure the bag near the bottom of the plant stem.
2. Set the plant in a place where it will get plenty of sunlight. Water the plant. Observe the inside of the plastic bag for five days. Record your observations each day.
3. On the fifth day, carefully remove the plastic bag. Measure the amount of water in the bag using the graduated cylinder. Record the amount of water that was collected in five days.

▲ **STEP 1** Cover the plant with a plastic bag.

Practicing Your Skills

4. **OBSERVE:** On which day did you first see water in the bag?
5. **COMPARE:** What happened to the amount of water in the plastic bag each day?
6. **INFER:** How much water did the plant give off in five days? Where did the water come from?

4-2 What is humidity?

Objective

Explain how we measure the amount of water vapor in the air.

Key Terms

capacity (kuh-PAS-ih-tee): amount of material something can hold

saturated (sach-uh-RAYT-ihd): filled to capacity

specific humidity (hyoo-MIHD-uh-tee): actual amount of water in the air

Humidity The amount of water vapor in a particular parcel of air is its humidity. High humidity means the air in that location contains a large amount of water vapor. Low humidity means that there is just a small amount of water vapor in the air in that location.

▲ **Figure 4-5** Water is always moving into or out of air.

1 DEFINE: What is humidity?

Capacity How much water can a 100-mL glass hold? If the glass is filled to the top, its capacity is 100 mL. **Capacity** is the amount of matter something can hold. The capacity of a 100-mL glass is always the same.

Air has a capacity for holding water vapor. Air's capacity for holding water vapor changes with the air temperature. As the temperature of the air goes down, air's capacity to hold water vapor goes down.

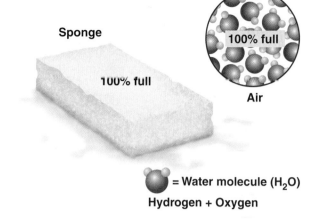

Sponge

100% full

100% full

Air

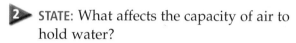
= Water molecule (H_2O)

Hydrogen + Oxygen

▲ **Figure 4-6** Air can be filled to capacity, just like this sponge.

2 STATE: What affects the capacity of air to hold water?

Saturated Air If you place a sponge in a pan of water, the sponge soaks up the water. Soon the sponge is filled with water. It cannot hold any more water. It is **saturated.** Air can be saturated, too. When air is saturated, it holds all the water vapor it can at a certain temperature. As the temperature goes up, the capacity of air for holding water goes up.

SATURATION OF AIR		
Temperature (°C)	(°F)	Grams of Water Vapor per Kilogram of Air
−40	−40	0.1
−30	−22	0.3
−20	−4	0.75
−10	14	2
0	32	3.5
5	41	5
10	50	7
15	59	10
20	68	14
25	77	20
30	86	26.5
35	95	35
40	104	47

▲ **Figure 4-7**

3 INFER: At which temperature will air hold more water vapor, 5°C or 25°C?

Specific Humidity The actual amount of water vapor that is in air is called **specific humidity.** Meteorologists express specific humidity as the number of grams of water vapor in 1 kg of air. Because specific humidity is measured by units of mass, it does not change with temperature or pressure. Only adding more water vapor to the air can change the specific humidity.

 NAME: How is specific humidity expressed?

✓ CHECKING CONCEPTS

1. The amount of _____ in the air is its humidity.
2. The amount of water vapor the air can hold is its _____.
3. The actual amount of water vapor in the air is called _____.
4. When air is _____, it holds all the water vapor it can at a given temperature.
5. The amount of water vapor that air can hold changes with _____.

💡 THINKING CRITICALLY

6. **INFER:** The air temperature in Boise, Idaho, is 25°C. The air temperature in Austin, Texas, is 35°C. Which city's air could hold more water vapor? Why?
7. **COMPARE:** How is a sponge similar to air in terms of capacity?

BUILDING SCIENCE SKILLS

Experimenting Obtain three different brands of paper towels. Take one sheet from each. Put water in a measuring cup, graduated cylinder, or marked beaker. Slowly saturate each towel with water and check to see how much water each towel held by how much is left in the cup. Which brand has the greatest capacity for holding water? Is it the most expensive brand? Compare quality to price for each towel.

 People in Science

METEOROLOGIST

During an airplane flight, a pilot radios to the tower to find out weather conditions. The pilot needs to know wind speed and direction, visibility, and cloud conditions. The pilot depends on weather information gathered by meteorologists.

Meteorologists are scientists who study the atmosphere and try to forecast the weather. They gather information about the atmosphere from hundreds of different places and at many altitudes. Weather satellites and computers also help meteorologists gather and analyze data.

▲ **Figure 4-8** A meteorologist checks all kinds of weather data.

Meteorologists work for the National Weather Service, airports, news bureaus, and farming organizations. Some work as weather broadcasters for TV or radio stations.

To be a meteorologist, you need a college education and a background in mathematics and science. The military services also offer special training programs in meteorology.

Thinking Critically What kinds of data do weather satellites gather?

4-3 How is relative humidity measured?

Objective
Explain relative humidity and how it is measured.

Key Terms
relative humidity: amount of water vapor in the air compared with the amount of water vapor the air can hold at capacity

psychrometer (sy-KRAHM-uht-uhr)**:** instrument used to find relative humidity

Relative Humidity The amount of water vapor in air compared with its capacity is **relative humidity.** The relative humidity of air that is saturated, or filled to its capacity, is 100 percent. Air is usually not filled to capacity. It may be filled to half its capacity. The relative humidity is then 50 percent.

The relative humidity of air changes as water vapor leaves the air and returns to the ocean or falls as precipitation. It also changes when water evaporates and goes into the air. If the amount of water vapor stays the same and the temperature drops, the relative humidity goes up. Relative humidity goes down if the temperature goes up.

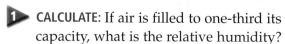 **CALCULATE:** If air is filled to one-third its capacity, what is the relative humidity?

Measuring Relative Humidity A **psychrometer** is sometimes used to find relative humidity. Figure 4-9 shows a simple psychrometer made up of two thermometers. The bulb of one thermometer is covered with a damp piece of cloth. The other bulb is dry. Air is then passed over the psychrometer. This causes water on the cloth to evaporate. The dry thermometer measures air temperature. Water evaporating from the cloth cools the wet thermometer. The wet thermometer is cooled more when the relative humidity is low than when it is high. Relative humidity can be found by using the difference in temperature between dry- and wet-bulb thermometers and a chart such as the one shown in Figure 4-10.

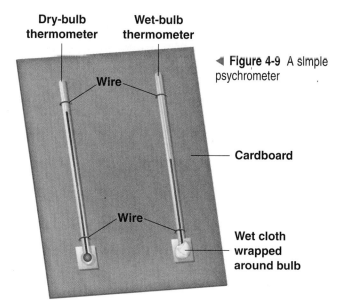

◀ **Figure 4-9** A simple psychrometer

Suppose the dry-bulb thermometer reads 25°C and the wet one reads 18°C. The difference is 7°C. Find 25°C along the top of Figure 4-10. Find 7°C down the left side. Where the two rows meet, you see the number 50. This means the relative humidity is 50 percent.

		Temperature of Air from Dry-Bulb Thermometer (°C)								
		-5	0	5	10	15	20	25	30	35
Difference Between Dry and Wet Thermometer (°C)	1	75	81	86	88	90	91	92	93	94
	2	52	64	72	77	80	83	85	86	87
	3	29	46	58	66	70	74	77	79	81
	4	6	29	46	55	62	66	70	73	75
	5		13	32	44	53	59	63	67	70
	6			20	34	44	51	57	61	70
	7			0	24	36	44	50	55	59
	8.				15	28	37	45	50	54

Relative Humidity (%)

▲ Figure 4-10

Another type of psychrometer is the sling psychrometer. This instrument can measure both relative humidity and dew point. The thermometers on this instrument are spun around until the temperature of the wet-bulb thermometer stops dropping.

 DEFINE: What is a psychrometer?

Humidity and Comfort As we perspire, moisture evaporates from our skin. The moisture evaporating from our bodies cools us. The faster the moisture evaporates, the cooler we feel. When the humidity is low, the rate of evaporation is faster. This makes us feel cooler. People living in a hot, dry climate may feel more comfortable than those in a cooler, moister climate. High relative humidity makes people feel uncomfortable. A temperature of 35°C with very low relative humidity may be quite comfortable. However, a temperature of 25°C with high relative humidity can be uncomfortable.

TEMPERATURE AND HUMIDITY IN THREE CITIES		
City	Temperature	Humidity
A	35°C	17%
B	35°C	62%
C	25°C	44%

▲ Figure 4-11

 INFER: What do you think an air conditioner does to the air temperature and humidity in a room?

✓ **CHECKING CONCEPTS**

1. The relative humidity of air filled to capacity at a given temperature is _____ percent.
2. The relative humidity goes up if the air temperature _____.
3. A _____ has two thermometers and is used to find relative humidity.
4. The relative humidity of air changes as _____ leaves the air.

THINKING CRITICALLY

5. **CALCULATE:** Use Figure 4-10 to find the relative humidity when the psychrometer readings are as follows: **a.** wet bulb, 12°C; dry bulb, 20°C; **b.** wet bulb, 33°C; dry bulb, 35°C; and **c.** wet bulb, 22°C; dry bulb, 30°C.

INTERPRETING VISUALS

Use Figure 4-11 to answer the following questions.

6. **INFER:** In which city would people be the most comfortable? The least comfortable?

 Hands-On Activity

EVAPORATION AND COOLING

You will need safety goggles, isopropyl (rubbing) alcohol, water, an index card, a stopwatch, and 2 cotton balls.

1. Gather your materials and put on the goggles. Fan your arm with an index card. Describe how it feels.
2. Dip a small cotton ball into some water and rub it on your arm. Fan the spot for 25 seconds. Describe how it feels.
3. Dip another cotton ball into some alcohol and rub this on your other arm. Fan this spot for 25 seconds. Describe how it feels.

▲ **STEP 1** Gather your materials.

Practicing Your Skills

4. **OBSERVE:** What happens to the water and to the alcohol when you fan your arm?
5. **EXPLAIN:** Why do evaporating liquids make your arm feel cooler?
6. **INFER:** Why do you feel cooler after you swim on a hot day?
7. **COMPARE:** Which evaporates faster, water or alcohol?
8. **INFER:** Why does sweating help to cool you down?
9. **HYPOTHESIZE:** Why do you feel warmer on a humid day?

4-4 What is the dew point?

Objective
Explain what happens when air temperature goes above or below the dew point.

Key Terms
condensation (kahn-duhn-SAY-shuhn)**:** changing of a gas to a liquid

dew point: temperature to which air must be cooled to reach saturation

frost: ice formed from condensation below the freezing point of water

Condensation Air always contains some water vapor. As the temperature of air drops, water vapor in the air changes from a gas to a liquid. The process of changing a gas to a liquid is called **condensation.**

Have you ever seen water form on the outside of a cold can or bottle? The water forms when water vapor in the air condenses into liquid water on the cold metal or glass.

▶ **1** **DESCRIBE:** What happens during the process known as condensation?

Dew Point The temperature of air at which condensation takes place is called the **dew point** of air. Condensation takes place when saturated air is cooled.

Warm air can hold more water vapor than cold air can. As the air cools, it can hold less and less water vapor. If the temperature of the air drops enough, the air becomes saturated. Its relative humidity reaches 100 percent.

If saturated air continues to be cooled, some of the water vapor in the air condenses. The water vapor changes to liquid water.

At night, the ground cools faster than the air. Air near the ground is then cooled by the ground. The temperature of the air may drop to or below its dew point. When this happens, condensation takes place. Drops of water called dew begin to form on grass and bushes. Dew may also form on the windows of cars.

▲ Figure 4-12 Dew forms on leaves when condensation occurs.

▶ **2** **DEFINE:** What is dew?

Frost The freezing point of water is 0°C. At this temperature, water changes from a liquid to a solid. When the humidity is low, the dew point of the air may be lower than the freezing point of water. If the air temperature drops below the dew point, water vapor will come out of the air. However, the water vapor will change directly to ice instead of water. Ice that forms this way is called **frost.**

▲ Figure 4-13 Frost forms if the air temperature drops below the freezing point and the dew point.

▶ **3** **HYPOTHESIZE:** Why doesn't frost form at temperatures above 0°C?

✓ CHECKING CONCEPTS

1. What is the process of condensation?
2. When does the process of condensation take place?
3. What is the dew point?
4. What happens to the relative humidity when the air becomes saturated?
5. What is the freezing point of water in the Celsius temperature scale?

💡 THINKING CRITICALLY

6. **APPLY:** Suppose condensation begins to form on the window of a car at 8°C. What is the dew point?
7. **EXPLAIN:** Why is the relative humidity of saturated air 100 percent?
8. **CONTRAST:** How do evaporation and condensation differ?
9. **HYPOTHESIZE:** How could you show that dew found on grass that is in direct sunlight evaporates quicker than dew found on grass that grows in the shade?

Web InfoSearch

Aircraft De-icing
One of the most dangerous things that can happen to an airplane is icing. Icing is caused by the freezing of so-called supercooled water droplets. Icing usually occurs on the wings and upper body of an airplane. The extra weight of the ice can reduce the ability of the airplane to fly. Airports usually de-ice airplanes, or melt the ice, during dangerous weather conditions.

▲ **Figure 4-14**
Plane being de-iced

SEARCH: Use the Internet to find out how ice affects airplanes. Also, how do airports de-ice an airplane? Start your search at **www.conceptsandchallenges.com**. Some key search words are **airplane deicing, airplane safety,** and **airplane disasters.**

Hands-On Activity

MEASURING DEW POINT

You will need an empty can, water, a cup of ice cubes, and a thermometer.

1. Fill a can about two-thirds full of water.
2. Place a thermometer into the water.
   ⚠ **CAUTION:** Do not let the bulb of the thermometer touch the bottom or sides of the can.
3. Add the ice cubes to the water. Observe the outside of the can. Record the temperature on the thermometer as soon as condensation appears on the outside of the can.

▲ **STEP 3** Observe the condensation on the outside of the can.

Practicing Your Skills

4. **MEASURE:** At what temperature did condensation appear on the can?
5. **IDENTIFY:** What are the water droplets that formed on the outside of the can called?
6. **IDENTIFY:** What is the name for the temperature at which condensation took place?
7. **APPLY:** What is the room's dew point?

4-5 How do clouds form?

Objectives
Describe how clouds form. Identify kinds of clouds.

Key Terms
cirrus (SIR-uhs) **cloud:** light, feathery cloud

cumulus (KYOO-myuh-luhs) **cloud:** big, puffy cloud

stratus (STRAYT-uhs) **cloud:** sheetlike cloud that forms layers across the sky

Cloud Formation From space, Earth sometimes seems to be covered with clouds. Clouds form from condensation in the atmosphere. Water droplets and ice form around dust and other particles in the air. Many billions of tiny water droplets and ice crystals form clouds. A cloud's shape is determined by how it formed.

 NAME: What process forms clouds?

Kinds of Clouds There are three basic kinds of clouds. Light, feathery clouds are called **cirrus clouds.** They are made up of ice crystals. They sometimes form at heights above 10,000 m.

Big, puffy clouds are called **cumulus clouds.** They form from rising currents of warm air that build to great heights. The base is usually flat.

Sometimes the sky is covered with a layer of sheetlike clouds. These are **stratus clouds.** Stratus clouds form layer upon layer, usually at low altitudes.

 LIST: What are the three basic kinds of clouds?

Fog A cloud that forms near the ground is fog. Fog forms from condensation. At night, the ground cools quickly. It cools the layer of air that lies above it. The air may be cooled to the dew point. If it is, the water vapor condenses and forms fog.

▲ **Figure 4-16** Fog rolls in off the ocean.

Thick blankets of fog can cover valleys or other low areas. Sometimes fog forms over rivers and lakes. This happens when cool air moves in over warm water.

 DESCRIBE: What is fog?

Cirrus

Cumulus

Stratus

◀ **Figure 4-15** Clouds come in three basic types: cirrus, cumulus, and stratus.

Cumulonimbus Clouds

Cumulonimbus clouds are cumulus clouds that are often associated with thunderstorms. Updrafts can raise a cumulonimbus

▲ **Figure 4-17** Cumulonimbus clouds are associated with thunderstorms.

cloud to heights taller than Mount Everest. As the clouds rise, their tops become flattened against the tropopause, the top of the troposphere. This large, flat top resembles a blacksmith's anvil. An anvil is a good indication that a thunderstorm is coming.

 COMPARE: How is a cumulonimbus cloud like a cumulus cloud?

✔ CHECKING CONCEPTS

1. What are clouds made of?
2. What are light, feathery clouds called?
3. What are sheetlike, layered clouds called?
4. What are three places you might see fog?
5. What kinds of clouds are large and puffy?

 THINKING CRITICALLY

6. **DESCRIBE:** Look outside at the sky. Are there clouds? What kind are they?
7. **MODEL:** Use cotton balls or wads of cotton to make models of the four kinds of clouds. Mount the clouds on a sheet of blue construction paper. Label the clouds.

Web InfoSearch

Thunderheads Another name for a cumulonimbus cloud is thunderhead. The sudden appearance of a thunderhead can mean that strong winds and heavy rains are on the way.

SEARCH: Use the Internet to find out more about thunderheads. How do they develop? How do meteorologists use them to learn more about the atmosphere? Start your search at www.conceptsandchallenges.com. Some key search words are **cumulus,** **cumulonimbus,** and **meteorology.**

 ## Science and Technology

CLOUD SEEDING

Imagine being able to make it rain on very hot days. How about making it snow so that you could go sledding or skiing? There is a way to do this. Cloud seeding can sometimes make it rain or snow.

In cloud seeding, crystals of carbon dioxide or silver iodide are dropped on clouds from high-flying airplanes. Ice crystals form around these crystals. The ice crystals grow until they become heavy and fall from the clouds. Whether it rains or snows depends on the air temperature.

▲ **Figure 4-18** Cloud seeding can sometimes make it rain or snow.

Cloud seeding can help prevent severe storms by causing it to rain before a storm grows too large. It can also help during droughts. However, cloud seeding does not work all of the time. Better technologies need to be developed to improve its success rate.

Thinking Critically Some people think that cloud seeding is like stealing. Farmers in one area that have the clouds seeded may be taking water from farmers in another area. What do you think?

LAB ACTIVITY
Making Cloud Models

Materials

Safety goggles

2-Liter soft drink bottle

Bicycle hand pump

Paper match

Water

Thermometer

BACKGROUND

Clouds are made from trillions of tiny water droplets. The droplets form around nearly invisible particles of dust, volcanic ash, and pollution.

PURPOSE

In this activity, you will investigate what is needed to make a cloud in a bottle.

PROCEDURE

1. Put on your goggles. Copy the chart in Figure 4-19 onto a clean sheet of paper.

2. For the first experiment, carefully slide the thermometer into the bottle. Screw on the cap with the thermometer still inside.

3. Have your teacher make a small hole in the bottle top. The hole should be just big enough for the hose of the bicycle hand pump to fit. Attach the hose of the bicycle pump to the cap of the cloud bottle. Make sure you have no air leaking out once you have the hose inserted into the bottle. Pump 10 to 20 times. Record the temperature.

4. Remove the hose. Observe what happens when you unscrew the cap and let the air out. Record the temperature again.

5. For the second experiment, add about a teaspoon of water to the bottle. Cap the bottle and shake it for about a minute. Record the temperature.

▲ **STEP 3** Pump air into the bottle.

▲ **STEP 5** Add a teaspoon of water to the bottle.

6. Attach the bicycle pump and pump the same number of times as in Step 3. Observe what happens when you unscrew the cap. Some water will still be in the bottle. Record the temperature.

7. For the third experiment, ask your teacher to light a paper match and blow it out. Your teacher should immediately drop the used match into the bottle to capture its smoke inside. Cap the bottle. Record the temperature.

8. Once again, attach the bicycle pump and pump the bottle as before. Observe what happens when you unscrew the cap. Record the temperature.

▲ **STEP 8** Attach the bicycle pump and pump the bottle again.

Making Clouds

Experiment	Temperature Before	Temperature After	What happened?
Air Only			
Water and Air			
Water, Smoke, and Air			

▲ **Figure 4-19** Use a copy of this chart for recording your observations.

CONCLUSIONS

1. **OBSERVE:** What happened to the temperature when you pumped air into the bottle? What happened when you released the pressure?

2. **OBSERVE:** In which experiment did you create the best cloud?

3. **INFER:** What are the parts of a cloud?

4. **ANALYZE:** How does air temperature affect cloud formation?

4-6 What is precipitation?

Objective
Identify and describe forms of precipitation.

Key Terms
precipitation (pree-sihp-uh-TAY-shuhn): water that falls to Earth from the atmosphere

rain gauge (GAYJ): device used to measure precipitation

Precipitation Conditions of the atmosphere vary greatly from place to place and season to season. This results in several different types of precipitation. **Precipitation** is water that falls to Earth from clouds. Precipitation may be a liquid or a solid. There are four major kinds of precipitation: rain, snow, sleet, and hail. All precipitation begins when water condenses in cool air.

▶ **LIST:** What are the four kinds of precipitation?

Rain, Snow, and Sleet Droplets of water and crystals of ice that make up clouds are very small. They are kept up in the air by air currents. The droplets of water are always moving. They hit into each other. When they hit, they join together. When they become too heavy, they fall as rain. Snow falls when ice crystals grow too heavy.

A very heavy snowstorm with strong winds and low temperatures is called a blizzard. During a blizzard, it is difficult to see. The heavy falling snow can block highways, airports, and railroad tracks.

Sometimes rain falls through cold layers of air. Sleet is rain that freezes as it falls through a layer of cold air near the ground.

Occasionally, the freezing of the rain doesn't occur until the rain strikes a surface near the ground. In this event, the rain forms a thick sheet of ice. When these conditions occur, it is called an ice storm.

▶ **CONTRAST:** How are rain and snow different?

Hail Hail is made up of lumps of ice. These lumps form as winds toss ice crystals up and down in a rain cloud. Each time the crystals move up, water freezes around them. These heavy lumps of ice eventually fall to the ground, often damaging property and crops. Hail usually occurs during strong thunderstorms.

▶ **OBSERVE:** What does a hailstone look like?

Measuring Precipitation A **rain gauge** is a device used to measure rainfall. Rain gauges collect water in one spot. The amount of rain that falls is usually measured in millimeters.

▲ **Figure 4-20** Precipitation can take many different forms.

Snow can also be measured with a rain gauge. The snow is collected, melted, and then measured. Snow depth is measured with a meter stick.

4 ▶ DEFINE: What is a rain gauge?

✓ CHECKING CONCEPTS

1. Precipitation may be a _____ or a solid.
2. There are _____ kinds of precipitation.
3. A liquid form of precipitation is _____.
4. Rain that freezes as it falls to Earth is called _____.
5. Snow depth is usually measured with a _____.

💡 THINKING CRITICALLY

6. **CLASSIFY:** What state of matter—liquid or solid—is each kind of precipitation?
7. **CONTRAST:** What is the difference between sleet and freezing rain?
8. **INFER:** What effect do you think an ice storm might have on tree branches?

Web InfoSearch

Cloud Forests
On the tops of mountains in Central America, hidden by mist, are the cloud forests. Trees in cloud forests are much shorter

▲ **Figure 4-21** A cloud forest in Central America

than lowland tropical trees. Their branches are usually covered with thick carpets of mosses, lichens, and ferns. Plants and animals in these high-elevation forests are like those in milder climates.

SEARCH: Use the Internet to find out more about cloud forests. How are they alike and different from rain forests? What species are found in there? Start your search at www.conceptsandchallenges.com. Some key search words are **cloud forests, mountains,** and **Central America.**

Hands-On Activity

MAKING A RAIN GAUGE

You will need safety goggles, a wide-mouthed jar, tape, and a ruler with both metric and inch markings.

1. Stand a ruler inside a wide-mouthed jar. Tape the ruler to the side of the jar.
2. Place the jar in an open area outdoors.
3. After it rains, measure the water in the jar. If it snows, allow the snow to melt. Measure in both inches and millimeters, then write down the numbers.
4. Compare your results with those listed in your local newspaper.

▲ **STEP 3** Write down your measurements in both inches and millimeters.

Practicing Your Skills

5. **INFER:** Why should a rain gauge be placed in an open area?
6. **a. COMPARE:** How did your readings compare with those listed in the newspaper?
   b. EXPLAIN: Were your readings and the newspaper readings of the weather different? Explain.
7. **INFER:** Why should you allow snow to melt before measuring it?

What are air masses?

Objective

Describe different kinds of air masses.

Key Terms

air mass: large volume of air with about the same temperature and amount of moisture throughout

polar air mass: air mass that forms over cold regions

tropical (TRAHP-ih-kuhl) **air mass:** air mass that forms over warm regions

Air Masses One day, it may be rainy. The next, it may be cloudy or sunny. To understand why weather changes, you need to know about air masses. An **air mass** is a large volume of air with about the same temperature and amount of moisture throughout. Air masses form when air stays over an area for a while or moves slowly over an area more than 1,000 km across.

An air mass is affected by the region it covers. Air masses that form over land are dry. Air masses that form over water are moist. Air masses that form over warm regions are warm. Those that form over cold regions are cold.

1 INFER: What is an air mass formed over the ocean in a cold region like?

Polar Air Masses Cold air masses that form over cold regions are called **polar air masses.** There are two kinds of polar air masses. The United States is affected by continental polar air masses that form over Canada. These are called continental polar air masses because the air mass forms over land. Continental polar air masses that form over Canada in the winter are very cold and dry.

Air masses that form over oceans in cold regions are moist. These air masses are called maritime polar air masses. The United States is affected by maritime polar air masses that form over the northern Pacific and Atlantic oceans.

2 NAME: What is a cold, dry air mass called?

Tropical Air Masses Warm air masses that form near the tropics are called **tropical air masses.** There are two kinds of tropical air masses. If they form over water, they are moist and warm. These are called maritime tropical air masses. The United States is affected by maritime tropical air masses that form over the oceans, the Caribbean Sea, and the Gulf of Mexico. Continental tropical air masses are warm and dry. They form over tropical land areas such as northern Mexico.

3 NAME: Where do warm, moist air masses in the United States form?

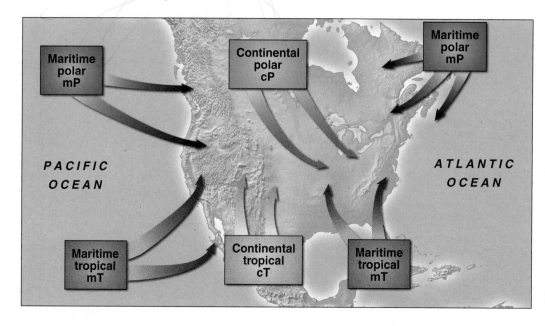

◀ Figure 4-22
Air masses over the United States

1. What is an air mass?

2. What is a warm, dry air mass called?

3. Does a continental polar air mass form over land or water?

4. What are the four main kinds of air masses?

5. What is a cold, moist air mass called?

THINKING CRITICALLY

Use Figure 4-22 to answer the following questions. Abbreviations are used to show the four kinds of air masses.

6. **APPLY:** Which type of air mass would be represented by mT?

7. **APPLY:** Which type of air mass is represented by cP?

8. **INFER:** What do you think the letters for a maritime polar air mass would be?

INTERPRETING VISUALS

Use Figure 4-23 below to do the following exercise.

9. **INFER:** Seven air masses affect the weather of North America. Four are tropical and three are polar. The air masses are listed below. Match them to the letters on the map.

Polar Pacific; polar Atlantic; tropical Pacific; tropical gulf; tropical Atlantic; polar Canadian; tropical continental

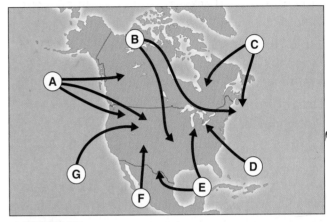

▲ Figure 4-23

How Do They Know That?

RIVERS OF AIR

Jet streams are rivers of fast-moving air. They can travel more than 300 km/h in a west-to-east direction. American pilots discovered the jet streams during World War II. Before then, planes were not equipped to reach the altitudes where jet streams occur. The World War II pilots were able to take advantage of the jet streams' high speeds to save fuel and time when traveling east. However, airplanes flying at high altitudes were slowed down when traveling west against the jet stream winds.

▲ Figure 4-24
Clouds in a jet stream

Jet streams form because of temperature and pressure differences. During winter, when there are greater variations in temperature, the jet streams are stronger.

Meteorologists often study jet streams with weather balloons. It appears that jet streams can strengthen and even change the movements of some weather systems. This affects the climate in some places. In India, for example, the jet stream is linked to the heavy monsoon rains.

Thinking Critically Why are jet streams weaker in the summer?

4-8 What is a front?

Objective
Describe the different kinds of fronts and the weather they cause.

Key Terms

front: boundary between air masses of different densities

cold front: forward edge of a cold air mass, formed when a cold air mass pushes under a warm air mass

warm front: forward edge of a warm air mass, formed when a warm air mass pushes over a cold air mass

Boundaries in Air A **front** is the boundary between two air masses of different densities. In the United States, air masses usually travel west to east. As they move, they meet up with other air masses.

Individual air masses do not usually mix. Instead, a front forms between them. A front can be hundreds of kilometers long. Fronts bring changes in the weather.

▲ **Figure 4-25** Fronts can be detected in satellite photos or sometimes by just looking up at the sky.

▶ **EXPLAIN:** What do fronts bring?

Cold Fronts A **cold front** is the forward edge of a cold air mass. A cold front is formed when a cold air mass pushes its way underneath a warm air mass.

Cold air is denser than warm air. As a cold front moves through an area, the warm air over a region is pushed upward. Gusty winds are formed because of differences in air pressure. Cold fronts usually bring rain and cloudy skies. Once the cold front passes, the cold air mass moves in.

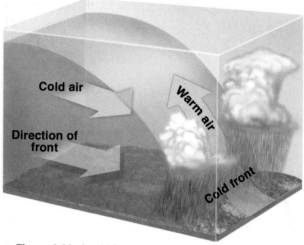

▲ **Figure 4-26** A cold front forms when cold air pushes warm air upward.

2 **DESCRIBE:** What kind of weather does a cold front bring?

Warm Fronts What happens when a warm front moves into an area? A **warm front** is the forward edge of a warm air mass. A warm front forms when a warm air mass pushes over a cooler air mass.

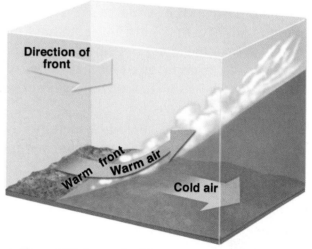

▲ **Figure 4-27** A warm front forms when a warm air mass pushes over cold air.

Warm air moves more slowly than cold air. Warm air rises above cold air. The rising warm air forms a gentle slope. The warm air slowly moves up and over the cold air. As the warm air rises, it cools. Cirrus clouds form high up, and precipitation may follow. Slow clearing and warmer temperatures show that a warm front has passed and the warm air mass has moved in.

3 ▶ **DEFINE:** What is a warm front?

Stationary Fronts Sometimes cold and warm air masses stay put for a while. They do not move. They remain stationary. This forms a stationary front. A stationary front brings very little change in the weather.

▲ **Figure 4-28** A stationary front brings little change in weather conditions.

4 ▶ **DEFINE:** What is a stationary front?

Occluded Fronts The most complex weather situation occurs with occluded fronts. In an occluded front, a warm air mass is between two cooler air masses.

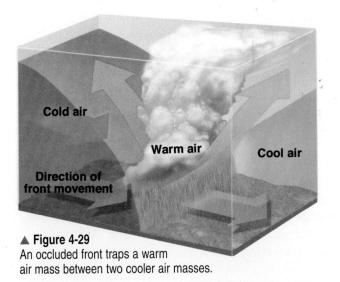

▲ **Figure 4-29**
An occluded front traps a warm air mass between two cooler air masses.

In an occluded front, the cooler air masses move beneath the warm air mass and push it up. They then come together in the middle and may mix. This makes the temperature near the ground cooler. The warm air mass is cut off, or occluded, from the ground. As the warm air cools and its water vapor condenses, the weather often turns cloudy, rainy, or snowy.

5 ▶ **DESCRIBE:** What happens to the weather with an occluded front?

✔ **CHECKING CONCEPTS**

1. What are four kinds of fronts?
2. How does a cold front form?
3. What kinds of clouds form when a warm front approaches?
4. Which kind of front causes very little change in weather?
5. What kind of weather is common with an occluded front?

💡 **THINKING CRITICALLY**

6. **INFER:** A city gets a day of rain and on the next day skies clear. The temperature rises. Which kind of front has passed?
7. **INFER:** If a city has clear skies and warm temperatures for three days, which kind of front might be keeping the weather the same?

Web InfoSearch

Tracking the Weather Go to the Internet to find out the weather report for three days. Keep a record of the fronts that are coming to your area. Write down the weather conditions that are forecast. Using that information, forecast the weather for the next two days. Check your forecast with current weather reports.

SEARCH: Start your search at www.conceptsandchallenges.com. Some key search words are **weather** and **fronts.**

What causes severe storms?

STEP 3

INVESTIGATE

Making a Boom
HANDS-ON ACTIVITY

1. Take a paper lunch bag and blow into it.

2. Close the open end of the bag with your hand, keeping the air inside.

3. With force, quickly hit the bag with your other hand.

THINK ABOUT IT: What happens when you hit the bag? What part of a storm does this noise remind you of? How do you think air was involved in making the sound?

Objective
Identify three kinds of severe storms.

Key Terms
thunderstorm: storm with thunder, lightning, and often heavy rain and strong winds

tornado (tawr-NAY-doh)**:** small, very violent, funnel-shaped cloud that spins

hurricane (HUR-ih-kayn)**:** tropical storm with very strong winds

Thunderstorms A **thunderstorm** is a storm with thunder, lightning, and often heavy rain and strong winds. Thunderstorms usually occur in summer, when a cold front forces warm, moist air to rise rapidly. Cumulus clouds build up to form cumulonimbus clouds. From these, heavy rain or hail falls.

▲ **Figure 4-30** Thunderstorms occur mostly along cold fronts.

Lightning occurs when a cloud discharges electricity. The current causes the air to heat and expand explosively. It creates a wave of compressed air. The wave produces the boom you hear as thunder. You see lightning flash before you hear thunder because light travels faster than sound does.

 DESCRIBE: What is a thunderstorm like?

Tornadoes A **tornado** is a funnel-shaped cloud that spins. Tornadoes cause very small, but very violent, storms. They frequently occur with severe thunderstorms. Tornadoes that form over water are called waterspouts.

Most tornadoes form during the spring or in early summer. Scientists are not sure how they form. They do know that a storm cloud may develop a small, spinning funnel that reaches down to the ground.

The funnel has very low air pressure. When it touches the ground, it acts like a giant vacuum cleaner, sucking everything up. As the funnel zigzags along, nearly all objects in its path are destroyed.

 DESCRIBE: What is a tornado?

Hurricanes A **hurricane** is a tropical storm with strong winds. These winds spiral toward the center. The winds may be stronger than 300 km/h.

People who study hurricanes may fly over or even into them to gather information. Most are scientists who work for the National Weather Service or the National Oceanic and Atmospheric Administration (NOAA).

From an airplane, the hurricane looks like bands of spinning clouds. The rain is heavy. The wind grows stronger and more destructive the closer you get to the eye of the storm. The eye is the calm, clear center of the storm. After the eye passes, the winds change direction.

▲ **Figure 4-31** Satellite photo of a hurricane

3 DESCRIBE: What is the eye of a hurricane like?

CHECKING CONCEPTS

1. When do thunderstorms usually happen?
2. What causes thunder?
3. What is the air pressure like in a tornado?
4. In what seasons do tornadoes usually form?

THINKING CRITICALLY

5. **INFER:** Not all the houses on a block may be damaged by a tornado. How can this be?
6. **CLASSIFY:** Which type of severe storm has each of these features? **a.** thunder and lightning **b.** funnel-shaped cloud **c.** giant cumulus clouds **d.** calm eye **e.** low air pressure

Web InfoSearch

Storms in History Many storms have changed history. Columbus and the passengers on the *Mayflower* met with severe storms. During World War II, one storm sank three U.S. naval destroyers and many smaller boats.

SEARCH: Use the Internet to find out more about this. How did storms affect Columbus's journey, World War II, and the *Mayflower* voyage? Start your search at www.conceptsandchallenges.com. Some key search words are **hurricanes, World War II,** and **voyages of Columbus.**

Real-Life Science

TORNADO ALLEY

More tornadoes occur in the United States than anywhere else on Earth. During some years, more than 800 tornadoes are counted in the United States. Most of these tornadoes form in the Great Plains and the southwestern United States. Oklahoma and Kansas have more tornadoes than most other states. This area of the United States is called the Tornado Belt or Tornado Alley.

In Tornado Alley, tornadoes occur most often in April, May, and June. Usually, they strike during the middle or late afternoon.

▲ **Figure 4-32** Tornadoes cause a great deal of destruction where they touch down.

The National Weather Service warns communities when dangerous thunderstorms are approaching. During a tornado, the best place to go is a basement or the lowest floor of a building. Crouch under a table or another heavy piece of furniture. Stay away from windows and doors. After the tornado passes, watch out for dangerous debris and damaged structures.

Thinking Critically Why do most thunderstorms form in late afternoon?

THE Big IDEA

How do electrical charges cause lightning?

Every atom of matter is made up of smaller particles of matter. Some of these particles, called protons, have a positive electrical charge. Other particles, called electrons, have a negative electrical charge.

If the number of protons and electrons is equal, the atom is neutral. This means that the atom lacks any electrical charge.

Rubbing an atom can cause it to lose some of its electrons. An example is when you drag your feet across a rug on a dry day. As your feet rub against the rug, they pick up electrons. As a result, your body has more electrons than protons. It carries an electrical charge. If you touch a metal object, the extra electrons travel through your fingers to the metal. The shock you feel is actually the movement of electrons.

Clouds that float above Earth's surface are made of water and ice. Temperature differences caused by the freezing of water droplets result in electrons being transferred between atoms. The clouds build up an electrical charge that is released as lightning.

Lightning can travel within a single cloud, between two clouds, or from a cloud to the ground. It can even travel from the ground to a cloud. When the electricity travels through the air, it causes the air to warm and expand quickly. The rapid expansion and then contraction of air molecules is heard as thunder.

Look at the illustrations on these two pages. Then, follow the directions in the Science Log to find out more about "the big idea." ✦

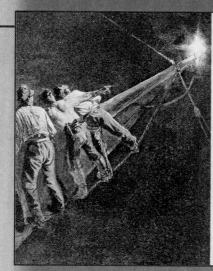

St. Elmo's fire
The sparks of light called St. Elmo's fire occur during a storm when not enough charges have built up to form a lightning bolt. Instead, a mass of sparks appears above the ground. This phenomenon was first noted above ships' mast, and so was named for the patron saint of sailors.

Cloud to Ground
In cloud-to-ground lightning, electrical charges flow from a cloud to Earth's surface. Some violent storms produce as many as 100 electrical charges per second. The air around can beome as hot as 30,000°C.

Cloud to Cloud
Lightning always travels along the path of least resistance. Usually, that means moving from one cloud to another.

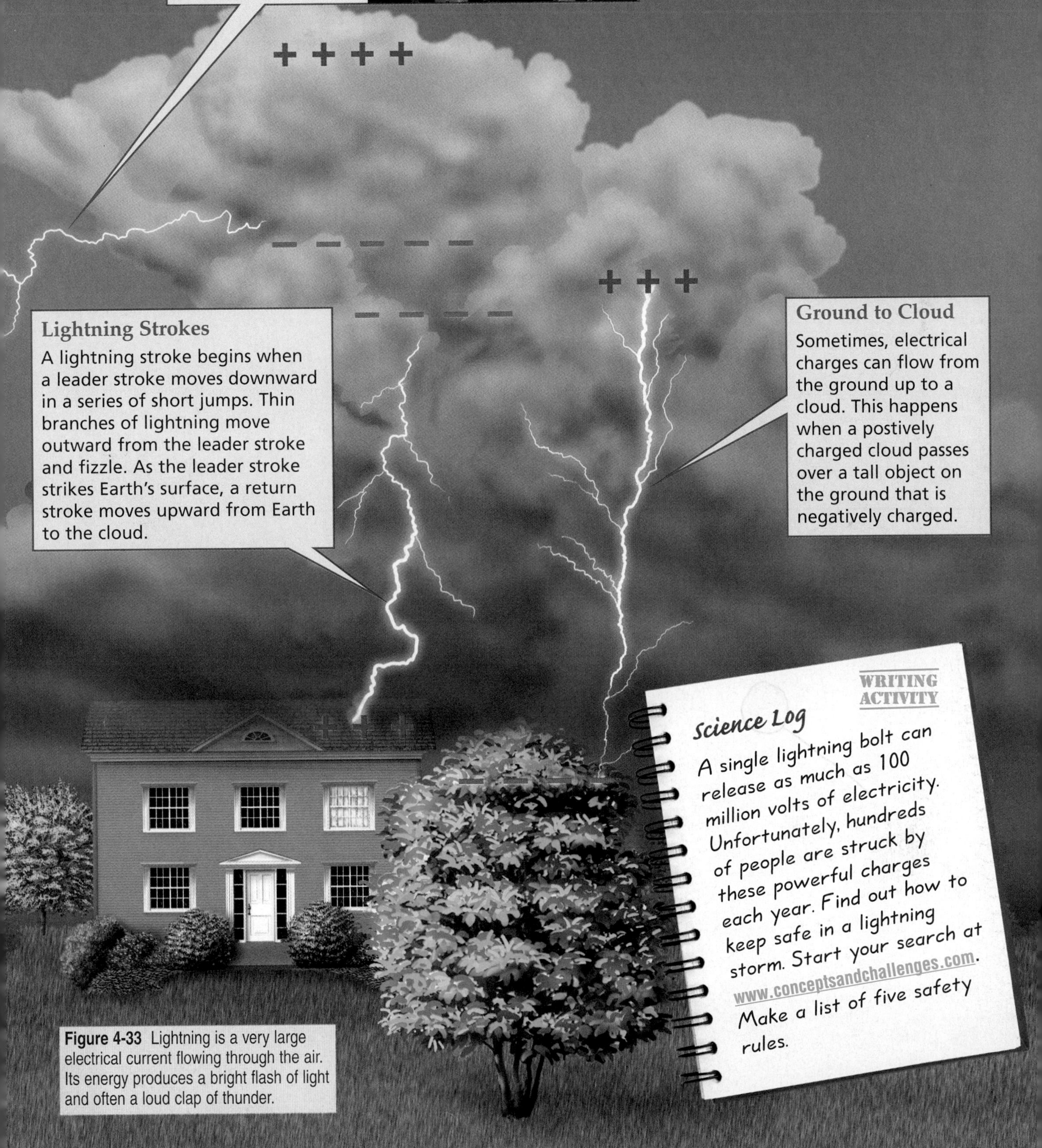

++++

– – – – –

+ + +

– – – – –

Lightning Strokes
A lightning stroke begins when a leader stroke moves downward in a series of short jumps. Thin branches of lightning move outward from the leader stroke and fizzle. As the leader stroke strikes Earth's surface, a return stroke moves upward from Earth to the cloud.

Ground to Cloud
Sometimes, electrical charges can flow from the ground up to a cloud. This happens when a postively charged cloud passes over a tall object on the ground that is negatively charged.

WRITING ACTIVITY

Science Log

A single lightning bolt can release as much as 100 million volts of electricity. Unfortunately, hundreds of people are struck by these powerful charges each year. Find out how to keep safe in a lightning storm. Start your search at www.conceptsandchallenges.com. Make a list of five safety rules.

Figure 4-33 Lightning is a very large electrical current flowing through the air. Its energy produces a bright flash of light and often a loud clap of thunder.

4-10 What is a station model?

Objective
Understand how to read a station model.

Key Terms
station model: record of weather information at a weather station

millibar (MIHL-ih-bahr)**:** unit of measurement for air pressure

Station Models A **station model** shows the weather conditions at a particular weather station. Station models such as the one in Figure 4-34 are used to depict weather conditions on a weather map. A station model uses symbols instead of words to describe weather. Each weather factor has a different symbol. Meteorologists, or weather scientists, use these symbols to make a station model.

Reading Station Models Each station model has a circle, which represents cloud cover. The amount of shading in the circle tells how much cloudiness there is. It is given in percentages. Figure 4-35 shows these percentages and their symbols. Symbols are also used for rain, snow, and other conditions.

Wind speed and direction are indicated on a station model with an arrow shaft leading to the station circle and small "feathers" sticking out at the end of this shaft. Look at Figure 4-35 for an example. The shaft is slanted in the direction from which the wind is coming. In the illustration, this is southwest. The length and number of feathers represent wind speed. Wind direction symbols are also given.

STATION MODEL

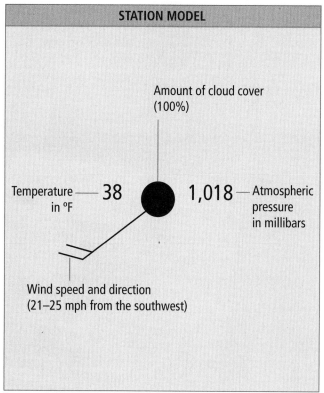

Amount of cloud cover (100%)

Temperature in °F — 38

1,018 — Atmospheric pressure in millibars

Wind speed and direction (21–25 mph from the southwest)

▲ Figure 4-34

STATION MODEL SYMBOLS			
Wind Speed (mph)	Symbol	Cloud Cover (%)	Symbol
1–2		0	
3–8		10	
9–14		20–30	
15–20		40	
21–25		50	
26–31		60	
32–37		70–80	
38–43		90	
44–49		100	
50–54			
55–60			
61–66			
67–71			
72–77			

▲ Figure 4-35

1 ▶ DEFINE: What is a station model?

2 ▶ OBSERVE: What is the wind speed on the station model shown in Figure 4-34?

Air Pressure In the United States, air pressure is measured in **millibars** (mb). A bar is a unit of pressure. It is based on the pressure created by a column of mercury that rises 750 mm at a temperature of 0°C. A millibar (mb) is a thousandth of a bar. Air pressure at the ground, or standard atmospheric pressure, is 1,013 mb.

Normal air pressure at ground level can range from 980 to 1,040 mb. The air pressure during a storm is usually lower than normal. From the outer edge of a hurricane to its center, air pressure can drop from over 950 mb to less than 800 mb. The lowest pressures ever recorded in the Western Hemisphere are associated with these storms. The steep drop in pressure creates the rapid, inward-spiraling winds of a hurricane. High pressure, on the other hand, usually brings with it clear, sunny skies.

 ANALYZE: What is the air pressure shown on the station model in Figure 4-34?

✔ CHECKING CONCEPTS

1. What does a station model show?
2. How can you tell how cloudy it is by looking at a station model?
3. How is wind direction shown on a station model?
4. How is the pressure measured?

 ## THINKING CRITICALLY

5. **MODEL:** Cut out a weather map from your local newspaper. Gather other weather information about your local area. Using the weather map and the information you are able to gather, draw a station model of your local area.

INTERPRETING VISUALS

Use the station model shown in Figure 4-34 to answer the following questions.

6. **INTERPRET:** From which direction is the wind blowing?
7. **INTERPRET:** How would you describe the cloud cover?
8. **INTERPRET:** What is the wind speed?

DESIGNING AN EXPERIMENT

Design an experiment to solve the following problem. Include a hypothesis, variables, a procedure with materials, and a type of data to study. Also tell how you would record the data.

PROBLEM: Suzie wants to collect data on the percentage of cloud cover in her neighborhood over a week's time. She will use the following materials to do so: a crayon, a ruler, and a large mirror. How can Suzie collect data using these materials?

 ## *Hands-On Activity*

READING A STATION MODEL

Examine the station models shown. Then answer the questions.

Practicing Your Skills

1. **DESCRIBE:** What is the sky condition for *A*?
2. **MEASURE:** What is the air pressure for *A* and *B*?
3. **OBSERVE:** What is the temperature for each?
4. **a. OBSERVE:** How fast is the wind blowing in each?
   b. IDENTIFY: From which direction is the wind blowing in each?
5. **INFER:** What kind of precipitation might be falling in *B*?
6. **MODEL:** Draw a station model that shows the conditions listed: **a.** air pressure, 1,018.8 mb; **b.** no cloud cover; **c.** temperature, 64°F; **d.** wind direction, from the southwest; **e.** wind speed, 35 mph.

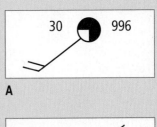

A

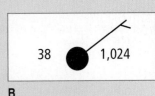

B

How do you read a weather map?

Objective

Read and interpret a weather map.

Key Terms

isobar (EYE-soh-bahr)**:** line on a weather map that connects points of equal air pressure

isotherm: line on a weather map that joins places that have the same temperatures

Weather Maps A weather map shows weather conditions for many places at one time. You can find the temperature, cloud cover, wind speed, and so on for many different locations. Data from more than 300 weather stations all over the country are assembled by the National Weather Service into weather maps each day. These maps are then used by newspapers and TV stations to prepare weather maps for their area.

▶ **1** **DEFINE:** What do weather maps show?

Reading a Weather Map Different weather maps can show different things. A key on a weather map helps you to read it. The pink lines that you see on the map in Figure 4-36 are called **isobars.** They connect points of equal air pressure. The numbers tell the pressure in millibars. Areas of high pressure are usually called highs. They are shown with an "H." Areas of low pressure are called lows. They are shown with an "L." On a different map, the pink lines might show isotherms. **Isotherms** are lines joining places that have nearly the same temperatures. Other symbols show fronts. Precipitation is shown as shading or with symbols like those in Figure 4-36.

▶ **2** **OBSERVE:** What was the temperature in Atlanta on the day this map was made?

Highs and Lows High-pressure regions have different weather than low-pressure regions. Highs usually bring clear skies. Lows usually bring cloudy skies and possibly precipitation.

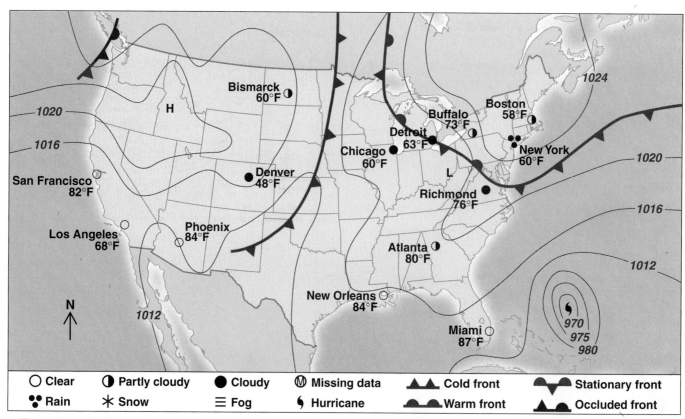

▲ **Figure 4-36** Weather map

Highs and lows usually move from west to east across the United States. As they pass through a region, they bring changes in the weather.

3 **DESCRIBE:** What type of weather does a low bring?

✔ CHECKING CONCEPTS

1. What are three weather conditions that you might find indicated on a weather map?

2. What do isobars show?

3. What are two ways to show precipitation on a weather map?

4. What do meteorologists usually call areas of low pressure?

5. What is the symbol weather maps use to indicate high pressure?

6. What do isotherms do?

💡 THINKING CRITICALLY

Use Figure 4-36 to do the following exercise.

7. **IDENTIFY:** Find a city that has each of the following weather conditions.

    a. clear skies
    b. cloudy
    c. partly cloudy
    d. highest temperature
    e. lowest temperature
    f. low air pressure
    g. inside a high

BUILDING SCIENCE SKILLS

Researching Many different symbols are used on weather maps. Do some research to find out some other weather symbols or different weather symbols for the same weather conditions. Draw and label the symbols on 3- × 5-inch index cards. What new symbols did you find? Make a list.

Real-Life Science

THE WEATHER PAGE IN A NEWSPAPER

Everyone is interested in the weather. Is it going to be sunny or stormy? Can we have our picnic? Will the ballgame be canceled? Weather has a big effect on our daily lives.

To find out the forecast, people often look in the newspaper. In it, you might find a four- to five-day local forecast, weather maps, a national forecast, and temperature graphs. Some newspapers contain a weather map for the local area. Others have a map of the country. Most newspapers have expected temperatures, in Fahrenheit. They also show fronts, precipitation data, and severe weather zones.

Temperature zones may be shaded in different colors. High- and low-pressure areas are indicated. Symbols for the fronts, steady rain, showers, flurries, and snow are shown. Some papers give average temperatures for that month. Others have the temperatures for different cities around the world.

Thinking Critically Why do newspapers have so much weather data?

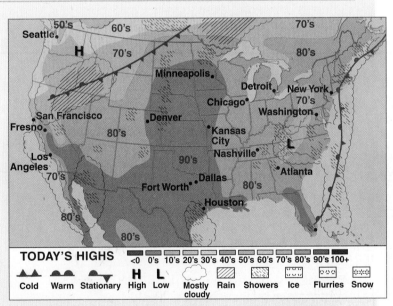

▲ **Figure 4-37** A typical newspaper weather map of the United States

Chapter 4 Challenges

Chapter Summary

Lessons 4-1, 4-2, and 4-3

- The gaseous form of water is water vapor. Most of the water vapor in the air evaporates from the oceans. Living things also add water to air. Humidity is the amount of water in the air.
- Air is **saturated,** or filled to **capacity,** when it holds all the water vapor it can at a given temperature.
- **Specific humidity** is the actual amount of water vapor in air. **Relative humidity** is the amount of water vapor in the air compared with what air can hold at full capacity. Temperature changes cause the relative humidity to change. A **psychrometer** is used to find relative humidity.

Lessons 4-4, 4-5, and 4-6

- When saturated air is cooled, **condensation** takes place. Water vapor condenses at the **dew point.**
- Saturated air cooled close to the ground forms dew. **Frost** forms when the dew point is below water's freezing point.
- Clouds form from condensation in the atmosphere. The three basic kinds of clouds are **cirrus, cumulus,** and **stratus.** Fog is a cloud that forms near the ground.
- Types of **precipitation** are rain, snow, sleet, and hail. Precipitation is measured with a **rain gauge.**

Lessons 4-7 through 4-11

- An **air mass** is a large volume of air with about the same temperature and moisture level throughout. **Polar air masses** form over cold regions. **Tropical air masses** form near the equator. Either can form over land or water.
- A **front** is where two air masses meet. Moving fronts cause weather changes. A **cold front** is the forward edge of a cold air mass. A **warm front** is the forward edge of a warm air mass.
- **Thunderstorms** include lightning, thunder, strong winds, heavy rains, and sometimes tornadoes. **Tornadoes** have funnel-shaped clouds that touch down on Earth's surface. A **hurricane** is a tropical storm with strong, spiraling winds.
- **Station models** describe local weather conditions. **Millibars** are units of air pressure.
- Weather maps show the weather for an area.

Key Term Challenges

air mass (p. 100)
capacity (p. 88)
cirrus cloud (p. 94)
cold front (p. 102)
condensation (p. 92)
cumulus cloud (p. 94)
dew point (p. 92)
evaporation (p. 86)
front (p. 102)
frost (p. 92)
hurricane (p. 104)
isobar (p. 110)
isotherm (p. 110)
millibar (p. 108)
polar air mass (p. 100)
precipitation (p. 98)
psychrometer (p. 90)
rain gauge (p. 98)
relative humidity (p. 90)
saturated (p. 88)
specific humidity (p. 88)
station model (p. 108)
stratus cloud (p. 94)
thunderstorm (p. 104)
tornado (p. 104)
transpiration (p. 86)
tropical air mass (p. 100)
warm front (p. 102)

MATCHING Write the Key Term from above that best matches each description.

1. process in which plants give off water
2. filled to capacity
3. line on a weather map that connects points of equal air pressure
4. small, violent, funnel-shaped cloud
5. temperature to which air must be cooled to reach saturation
6. amount of matter something can hold
7. unit of measurement for air pressure
8. record of weather data at a weather station

APPLYING DEFINITIONS Explain the difference between the words in each pair. Write your answers in complete sentences.

9. evaporation, condensation
10. cirrus cloud, stratus cloud
11. air mass, front
12. thunderstorm, hurricane
13. humidity, specific humidity
14. cold front, warm front
15. frost, precipitation
16. isobar, isotherm

Content Challenges TEST PREP

MULTIPLE CHOICE Write the letter of the term or phrase that best completes each statement.

1. Light, feathery clouds are called
   a. cirrus clouds.
   b. cumulus clouds.
   c. stratus clouds.
   d. nimbus clouds.

2. Each station model is marked by a
   a. word.
   b. circle.
   c. square.
   d. triangle.

3. In the United States, air pressure is measured in
   a. millibars.
   b. meters.
   c. milliliters.
   d. kilograms.

4. If air is filled to half its capacity, the relative humidity is
   a. 100 percent.
   b. 75 percent.
   c. 50 percent.
   d. 25 percent.

5. Fog forms over rivers and lakes when cool air moves in over
   a. cold water.
   b. warm water.
   c. warm air.
   d. cirrus clouds.

6. Air masses do not usually
   a. form fronts.
   b. move.
   c. mix.
   d. meet.

7. Tornadoes usually form during
   a. early winter.
   b. late fall.
   c. early summer.
   d. late winter.

8. Most of the water in the air evaporates from
   a. the oceans.
   b. the soil.
   c. puddles.
   d. lakes and rivers.

FILL IN Write the term or phrase that best completes each statement.

9. As temperature drops, the capacity of air for holding water goes _____.

10. Molecules in a liquid are always _____.

11. Air masses that form over oceans are _____.

12. Standard air pressure is about _____ millibars.

13. As the temperature of the air reaches the dew point, water vapor changes from a gas to a _____.

14. Lightning is caused when giant storm clouds discharge _____.

15. The way a cloud forms gives it its _____.

16. A front brings changes in the _____.

17. Relative humidity goes _____ if the temperature drops.

18. There is no wind or rain in the _____ of a hurricane.

WRITTEN RESPONSE **Answer each of the following questions in complete sentences.**

1. **RELATE:** How are specific humidity and relative humidity related?

2. **CONTRAST:** What is the difference between sleet and hail?

3. **EXPLAIN:** Why does a cold air mass push under a warm air mass?

4. **EXPLAIN:** Why is the wet thermometer of a psychrometer cooled more when the relative humidity is low than when it is high?

5. **APPLY:** How do different air masses affect the weather in the United States?

6. **RELATE:** How does the process of changing a liquid to a gas relate to different forms of weather?

7. **EXPLAIN:** How is specific humidity measured?

8. **EXPLAIN:** How are each of the four kinds of precipitation formed?

9. **INFER:** The grass outside in the morning is wet, and it has not rained. What process probably took place to cause the dew?

INTERPRETING VISUALS **Use Figure 4-38 below to answer the following questions.**

10. What is the relative humidity when the dry thermometer reads 5°C and the wet thermometer reads 0°C?

11. What is the relative humidity when the dry thermometer reads 20°C and the wet thermometer reads 13°C?

12. If the relative humidity is 50 percent and the dry thermometer reads 30°C, what does the wet thermometer read?

		Temperature of Air from Dry-Bulb Thermometer (°C)							
		-5	0	5	10	15	20	25	30	35
Difference Between Dry and Wet Thermometer (°C)	1	75	81	86	88	90	91	92	93	94
	2	52	64	72	77	80	83	85	86	87
	3	29	46	58	66	70	74	77	79	81
	4	6	29	46	55	62	66	70	73	75
	5		13	32	44	53	59	63	67	70
	6			20	34	44	51	57	61	70
	7			0	24	36	44	50	55	59
	8				15	28	37	45	50	54

Relative Humidity (%)

▲ Figure 4-38

Chapter 5 Climate

▲ **Figure 5-1** Tree trunks reveal changes in climate over the years. This cross section is from an Acacia tree.

Contents

Look at a cross section of a tree trunk. You should see a series of bands or rings. Starting in spring, the trunks of trees grow by producing bands of new material just beneath the bark. The bands produced in late summer look darker. This forms a pattern of rings. One combined ring represents one year of a tree's life. Rings provide a clue to climate. In good weather, there is more growth. That means the darker bands will be wider.

►About how old was the tree that produced the trunk in this picture?

5-1 What is climate?

Objectives

Explain how weather and climate are related.
Identify the factors that determine climate.

Key Terms

weather: day-to-day conditions of the atmosphere

climate (KLY-muht): average weather conditions of an area over many years

Weather and Climate Air temperature, the appearance of the sky, winds, and the amount of moisture in the air all are part of weather. **Weather** is the day-to-day conditions of the atmosphere. The average weather conditions of an area from year to year is its **climate.** Climate describes the weather patterns of an area over time.

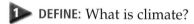 **DEFINE:** What is climate?

Average Temperatures Average monthly and yearly temperatures can be used to describe climate. The monthly average is found by adding together the daily average temperature for each day of the month and dividing by the number of days in the month. The yearly average temperature is a total of the twelve monthly averages divided by twelve.

▶ **DESCRIBE:** How do you find daily average temperature?

Temperature Range How much the temperature changes during the year is also important in describing climate. This is temperature range. To find the temperature range, subtract the lowest monthly average temperature from the highest. In Eureka, California, for example, the average monthly temperature for July is 14°C. In January it is 9°C. In New York City, the average monthly temperature goes from 25°C in July to about −6°C in January. New York City has a greater temperature range than Eureka does. The temperature range for Eureka is 5°C. New York City has a temperature range of 31°C. Eureka and New York City have different climates partly because they have different temperature ranges.

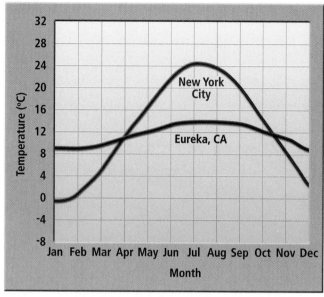

▲ **Figure 5-2** Average monthly temperatures for New York City and Eureka, California

▶ **INFER:** Does New York City or Eureka have a colder climate?

Average Precipitation Average monthly precipitation is also used to describe climate. Precipitation is rain, snow, sleet, or hail. Average monthly precipitation is the average amount of water from rain, snow, sleet, or hail that falls in an area in a month. It is measured in centimeters or inches.

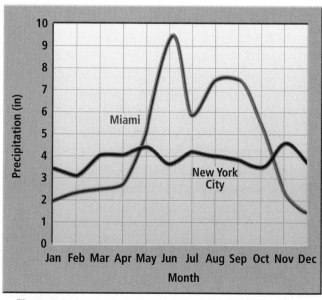

▲ **Figure 5-3** Average monthly precipitation for New York City and Miami, Florida, over a thirty-year period.

However, average precipitation is not enough to describe climate. Both Miami, Florida, and New York City get moderate amounts of precipitation yearly. However, Figure 5-3 shows that in New York City, precipitation falls steadily throughout the year. New York City gets rain, snow, sleet, and hail. In Miami, the most rain falls during a rainy season. The rainy season is May through October. Miami usually does not get snow or sleet. New York City and Miami have very different climates.

 INFER: Which has a colder climate, Miami or New York City? Explain.

✓ CHECKING CONCEPTS

1. The condition of the atmosphere today is the _____.

2. The _____ of an area describes the average weather conditions from year to year.

3. Temperature _____ describes the yearly change in temperature.

4. Rain and snow are two different kinds of _____.

THINKING CRITICALLY

5. **CALCULATE: a.** The high temperature in Chicago was 12°C. The low was 8°C. What was the temperature range that day? **b.** The high temperature in Houston was 25°C. The low was 21°C. What was the average temperature in Houston that day?

6. **INFER:** What two factors have the greatest effect on climate?

BUILDING SCIENCE SKILLS

Comparing and Contrasting In warm, dry climates, people usually wear loose-fitting, light colored, lightweight clothing. In cooler climates, they wear snug-fitting clothing and dark colors. Find out about the kinds of clothing that are appropriate to each kind of climate. What fabrics are best? How do the clothing styles of different cultures relate to their climates? Write a brief report on the relationship between clothing and climate.

 How Do They Know That?

THE LOST COLONY OF GREENLAND

In A.D. 985, during a warm period, Erik the Red led an expedition to Greenland from Iceland. As a result, two small Norse settlements were established on the western coast. By the early twelfth century, there were about 5,000 people living there. They had cattle, sheep, and goats. There was plenty of wildlife. The colonists received supplies from Iceland and Scandinavia regularly.

Later that century, the weather in Greenland cooled sharply. This cooling of temperature was ahead of any climate change in Europe. The following century was even colder. These changes caused more frequent storms. More pack ice grew around the island. Visits from Icelanders decreased. By the late 1400s, both settlements had died out completely. One possible cause was malnutrition. This is the only recorded example of an established European society being completely wiped out.

Thinking Critically How did the change in climate cause the settlements to disappear?

▲ **Figure 5-4** Traces of the lost settlements of Greenland are still found there today.

What factors determine climate?

Objective

Identify and describe the conditions that determine climate.

Key Terms

latitude (LAT-uh-tood)**:** distance north or south of the equator in degrees

altitude (AL-tuh-tood)**:** height above sea level

Latitude The climate of an area is affected by its latitude. **Latitude** is the distance in degrees north or south of the equator. Latitude determines how much heat energy an area gets from the Sun. At the equator, the Sun's rays fall almost directly on Earth. The closer an area is to the equator, the warmer is its climate. At higher latitudes, the Sun's rays strike Earth at more of an angle. The heat energy from the Sun is spread out, and the climate is colder. Global wind patterns at different latitudes also alter the number and kinds of storms in an area.

▶ **RELATE:** How does latitude affect climate?

Altitude The height above sea level is called **altitude.** Air is warmer at sea level than it is at higher altitudes. The average air temperature drops about 1°C for every 100-m rise in altitude. Even near the equator, mountaintops are snow-covered all year.

▲ **Figure 5-5** This picture shows the kinds of vegetation that can be found at different altitudes, from mountaintop to sea level.

▶ **DEFINE:** What is altitude?

Ocean Currents Ocean currents have an effect on the climate of areas along the seacoast. An ocean current is like a river of water within the ocean. Some ocean currents are warm. Other ocean currents are cold. Winds passing over ocean currents are either warmed or cooled by them. When these winds reach nearby land areas, they heat or cool the land.

 DESCRIBE: How do ocean currents affect land temperatures?

Mountains When air passes over a mountain range, the air rises and cools. The side on which the air rises is called the windward side. Moisture condenses from the cooled air, causing it to either rain or snow.

As the air moves down the other side of the mountain, the leeward side, it is warmed and most of the moisture is removed. It rarely rains on the leeward side of a mountain. Many deserts, such as Death Valley, are found on the leeward sides of mountains. These areas are sometimes called rain shadow deserts.

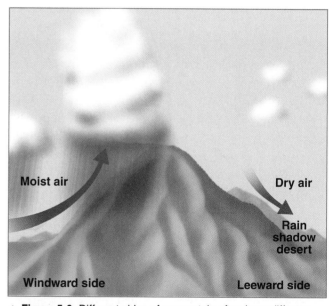

Moist air   Dry air

Rain shadow desert

Windward side   Leeward side

▲ **Figure 5-6** Different sides of a mountain often have different weather patterns.

 OBSERVE: What side of a mountain faces the wind?

1. The closer an area is to the equator, the _____ its climate.

2. At _____ latitudes, the Sun's rays strike Earth at more of an angle.

3. Air at sea level is _____ than air at higher altitudes.

4. Land areas near cold-water currents usually have _____ temperatures.

THINKING CRITICALLY

5. **CALCULATE:** How much lower will the temperature be on top of a 1,500-m mountain than at sea level?

6. **INFER:** Miami, Florida, is at a lower latitude than San Francisco, California. Which city probably has a warmer climate? Explain.

Web InfoSearch

The Butterfly Effect There are many factors influencing the weather. A change in any one can affect the others in unpredictable ways. This is chaos theory. Weather patterns do repeat over the years. This is climate. However, past patterns are never repeated exactly. This is partly the result of the butterfly effect, which is the idea that a butterfly's wings stirring the air in one place can lead to large storms a month later far away.

SEARCH: Use the Internet to find out more about chaos theory. What besides the weather does it affect? Start your search at www.conceptsandchallenges.com. Some key search words are **chaos theory, climate change,** and **weather patterns.**

Real-Life Science

THE RAINIEST PLACES ON EARTH

You might think that the rain forests are the rainiest places on Earth. They do get more than 150 cm of rain per year. Some get up to 1,000 cm each year. Where could it rain more than that?

Actually, some of the rainiest places on Earth are found on windward mountain slopes. Mount Waialeale (wy-ahl-ay-AHL-ay) in Hawaii gets 1,150 cm per year, the highest average annual rainfall in the world. Cherrapunji (cher-uh-PUN-jee), India, is second, with about 1,125 cm a year. Cherrapunji holds the record for the most rainfall in one year, at 2,605 cm. Most of this rain fell in one month, July. Compare this with Seattle, Washington, which is known for its rainy weather. The average rainfall there is about 98 cm per year.

▲ Figure 5-7 Mt. Waialeale in Hawaii has the highest annual rainfall in the world.

Mountain areas get a lot of rain and snow. Runoff from mountains such as the Rockies can be a source of water for dry areas in the southwestern United States. Reservoirs in mountain areas can store spring runoff. This water can then be delivered to Los Angeles and other cities by a network of canals.

Thinking Critically What is the average monthly rainfall in Mt. Waialeale, Hawaii?

5-3 What are climate zones?

INVESTIGATE

Reading a Climograph
HANDS-ON ACTIVITY

1. Climographs allow scientists to compare different weather conditions to see if they are related. For example, scientists might compare hours of daylight and temperatures. Look at the climograph in Figure 5-8. In it, total rainfall and average monthly temperatures are compared.

2. Observe which month is warmest.

3. Observe which month has the most rainfall.

THINK ABOUT IT: Are precipitation and temperature related in Kansas City, Missouri? How can you tell?

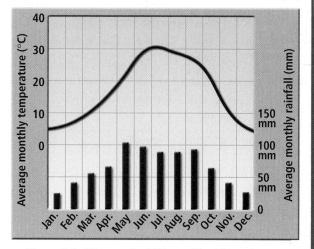

▲ **Figure 5-8** Climograph of Kansas City, Missouri

Objective
Identify and describe the three main climate zones.

Key Terms
tropical (TRAHP-ih-kuhl) **zone:** warm region near the equator

polar zone: cold region above 60°N and below 60°S latitude

middle-latitude zone: region between 30° and 60°N and S latitude

Latitudes and Climate Zones A climate zone is an area of Earth that has a certain temperature range and similar weather conditions. Figure 5-9 on the next page shows the three main climate zones. The warm zone near the equator is the **tropical zone.** It is between 30°N and 30°S latitude. The average monthly temperature is 18°C or higher. The coldest climate zones are the **polar zones.** These are above 60°N and below 60°S latitude. Temperatures do not go above 10°C. Between 30° and 60°N and S latitude are the **middle-latitude zones.** The temperature in the coldest months in these places averages no less than 10°C. The warmest month averages no colder than 18°C.

▶ **DEFINE:** What is a climate zone?

Solar Energy and Climate Zones The biggest influence on climate and weather is energy from the Sun. The amount of solar energy received at a particular spot is determined by the tilt of Earth on its axis. This tilt influences the angle at which sunlight strikes Earth.

Climate conditions and weather are affected by how directly the Sun's rays strike an area. The Sun's rays are most direct and have the greatest effect at the equator. The places on Earth closest to the equator have the warmest climates.

Because Earth's poles get the least amount of sunlight, they are the coldest places on Earth. In between, it depends on the seasons. Other factors that can affect the climate of a region include topography, location of lakes and oceans, availability of moisture, global wind patterns, ocean currents, and location of air masses.

▶ **ANALYZE:** What state in the United States has long, cold winters and short, warm summers?

Rainfall and Climate Zones In each climate zone, there are many smaller climate zones based on rainfall. In the tropics, climates may be very arid, or dry. They can also be very humid, or wet. In the polar zones, the climate is always cold and never humid. The middle-latitude zones have many different climates.

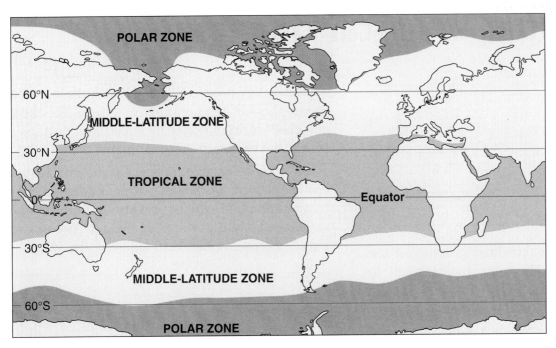

POLAR ZONE

60°N

MIDDLE-LATITUDE ZONE

30°N

TROPICAL ZONE

0°   Equator

30°S

MIDDLE-LATITUDE ZONE

60°S

POLAR ZONE

◀ **Figure 5-9** The three main climate zones are the tropical, middle-latitude, and polar zones.

The importance of climate cannot be overestimated. In addition to its effects on human life, climate determines the type of soil and vegetation found in a given area. This, in turn, determines how the land supports living things.

3 **ANALYZE:** What creates smaller climate zones within the larger ones?

☑ CHECKING CONCEPTS

1. Earth is divided into _____ climate zones.
2. Places with the coldest temperatures are located in the _____ zone.
3. Places with the warmest temperatures are located in the _____ zone.
4. The middle-latitude zone has many different combinations of _____ and amounts of rainfall.
5. The middle-latitude zone is located between _____ N and S latitude.

💡 THINKING CRITICALLY

6. **IDENTIFY:** Using Figure 5-9, indicate the lines of latitude that separate the tropical zone from the middle-latitude zones.

INTERPRETING VISUALS

Copy the table in Figure 5-10 onto a sheet of paper. Look at the three cities listed and their locations. Use the terms warm, moderate, *and* cold *to fill in the column titled "Type of Climate." Study the list of temperatures. Match each city with its temperature. Write the numbers in the table. Then, answer the questions.*

LATITUDE AND CLIMATE				
City	Location (Latitude)	Type of Climate	Average Temperature	
			January	July
Singapore	1°N			
Pt. Barrow, AK	71°N			
Boston, MA	42°N			

▲ **Figure 5-10**

Coldest Month
January average: 78°F
January average: 30°F
January average: −11°F

Warmest Month
July average: 79°F
July average: 73°F
July average: 44°F

7. **EXPLAIN:** Why are regions close to the equator (0° latitude) warmer than those far from the equator?
8. **CALCULATE:** What is the yearly temperature range for each city listed in your table?

5-4 What are local climates?

Objective
Describe some factors that affect local climates.

Key Term
microclimate (MY-kroh-kly-muht): very small climate zone

Local Climate Local conditions can affect the climate of any area. These conditions result in small climate zones called local climates.

Altitude, or distance above sea level, has the greatest effect on local climates. Large lakes and forests also affect local climates. Like oceans, large lakes can warm or cool the temperature of the air. Forests are another factor. They slow down winds and add water vapor to the air. This increases humidity.

▲ **Figure 5-11** Large lakes can cool or warm the air temperature of nearby regions.

▶ IDENTIFY: What are three factors that can affect local climates?

Microclimates Local climates can be broken down into even smaller climate zones. These very small climate zones are called **microclimates**. A microclimate can be as small as a schoolyard.

All cities have microclimates. The average temperature in a city is higher by several degrees than it is in surrounding areas. Heavy traffic in cities warms the air and raises average temperatures.

The energy used to heat and light buildings also raises the air temperature in cities. The heat absorbed during the day by streets and buildings is radiated back into the air at night.

Skyscrapers in cities may act as mountains and change patterns of rainfall. Air pollution and dust from automobile exhaust and also from industrial smokestacks add particles to the air. These extra particles cause more rain to fall over large cities.

▲ **Figure 5-12** Tall buildings, such as skyscrapers in New York City, create city microclimates.

▶ EXPLAIN: How do skyscrapers affect the climate in cities?

Global Warming Climate has changed many times during Earth's history. These changes were mostly due to natural causes. Today, human activities may be changing Earth's climate. Increased air pollution may cause temperatures around the world to increase. This pattern of increased temperature is called global warming.

Global warming could cause the polar ice caps to melt. Sea levels might rise as much as 60 m. New York City would be almost covered with water. Only the tops of very tall buildings would be above the water.

3 **PREDICT:** What would New York City look like if the ice caps melted?

✓ CHECKING CONCEPTS

1. What factor affects local climates the most?

2. Is the average temperature in a city lower or higher than that of surrounding areas? Why?

3. Can air pollution affect the amount of rainfall in an area? Explain.

4. What is global warming?

💡 THINKING CRITICALLY

5. **HYPOTHESIZE:** Chicago is located in the north central United States. It is on one of the Great Lakes. How does this affect the local climate?

6. **INFER:** Would you expect a city or its suburbs to get more snow? Explain.

Web InfoSearch

The Greenhouse Effect Earth's surface is surrounded by gases. Some of these gases trap heat from the Sun. Without these so-called greenhouse gases, Earth would be much colder. The warming that occurs is known as the greenhouse effect.

In the last few centuries, people have been burning wood, coal, oil, and gasoline for fuel. This has released huge amounts of carbon dioxide into the atmosphere. Carbon dioxide is a greenhouse gas. The burning of wood and fossil fuels is thought to be a major cause of global warming.

SEARCH: Use the Internet to find out more about the greenhouse effect. Will Earth continue to warm up? If so, what changes could occur? Start your search at www.conceptsandchallenges.com. Some key search words are **greenhouse effect, carbon dioxide, greenhouse gases,** and **global warming.**

 How Do They Know That?

LONG-TERM CLIMATE TRENDS

Changes in the surface temperatures of ocean water can cause long-term changes in climate. These changes could explain sudden climate shifts, such as the Little Ice Age. The Little Ice Age was a cold period from about 1450 to 1850 that included many harsh winters in Europe.

Climate changes may occur because ocean water is always on the move. Scientists see the ocean as a kind of giant conveyor belt that moves and mixes water in a never-ending cycle around the globe.

Cold, salty water sinks into the deep ocean in the North Atlantic. The water flows south and then east around southern Africa. There, the water rises again to the surface. This water is then warmed in the Indian and Pacific oceans. Surface currents carry the warmed water back through the Pacific and South Atlantic oceans. The round trip takes between 500 and 2,000 years.

Thinking Critically How can ocean currents affect climate?

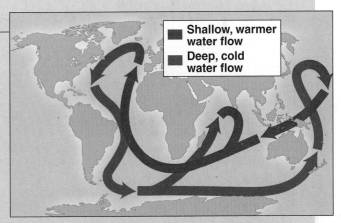

■ Shallow, warmer water flow
■ Deep, cold water flow

▲ **Figure 5-13** Ocean water makes a never-ending roundtrip journey around the world.

LAB ACTIVITY
Investigating How Land Surface Affects Air Temperature

Materials

Safety goggles
Lab apron
3 Paper or foam plates
3 Thermometers
Aluminum foil
Dark rock or pieces
   of asphalt
Grass sod
Light-colored sand

▲ **STEP 1** Pour sand into one plate.

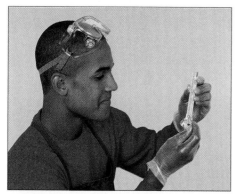

▲ **STEP 3** Use foil to cover your thermometer bulbs.

BACKGROUND

Year round, cities are warmer than suburbs and rural areas. When land is cleared of trees to make way for roads, buildings, and parking lots, the local climate is changed.

PURPOSE

In this activity, you will investigate the relationship between air temperature and land surface.

PROCEDURE

1. Prepare three plates for your experiment. Cover one plate with grass sod. Cover another plate with dark-colored rock or asphalt. Cover the last plate with light-colored sand.

2. Copy the chart in Figure 5-14.

3. Cover the end, or bulb, of each thermometer with aluminum foil. Take the plates outside and place them in the sunlight. Hold your thermometer 2.5 cm above the middle of each plate. In your chart record the temperatures.

4. Measure and record the temperatures again 5 minutes later.

5. Measure and record the temperatures after 10 minutes.

6. Measure and record the temperatures after 15 minutes.

7. Take your plates out of the sunlight, so that they can start to cool. In your chart, below the first group of numbers, record the temperatures after 5, 10, and 15 minutes for each plate.

STEP 7 ▶
Take the temperatures above the three plates as they cool.

Air Temperature and Land Surfaces			
Time Outdoors	Temperature above dark surface	Temperature above grassy surface	Temperature above light surface
0 minutes			
5 minutes			
10 minutes			
15 minutes			
Cooling Times			
0 minutes			
5 minutes			
10 minutes			
15 minutes			

▲ **Figure 5-14** Use a copy of this chart to record the temperatures.

CONCLUSIONS

1. **OBSERVE:** Which plate had the highest temperature?

2. **OBSERVE:** Which plate had the lowest temperature? Which cooled fastest? Which stayed warmer the longest?

3. **INFER:** Why was there a difference?

4. **ANALYZE:** How could cities be changed to make them cooler?

How does climate affect living things?

Objective
Identify ways in which plants and animals are affected by climate.

Key Terms
biome (BY-ohm): large region with a characteristic climate and plant and animal communities

vegetation (vehj-uh-TAY-shuhn): plants

Biomes   A large region with a characteristic climate and certain kinds of living things is called a **biome.** Scientists identify a biome mainly by the major types of plants growing in the area. Because many animals eat only certain kinds of plants, each biome also has a particular group of animals and other organisms living there.

▶ **1** **IDENTIFY:** How do scientists identify a biome?

Climate and Vegetation   Climate affects the vegetation in an area. **Vegetation** refers to the plants in an area. Rainfall and temperature are the climate factors that most affect vegetation.

Some kinds of plants need a lot of water. For example, many species of trees grow only in tropical rainy climates. Some plants grow where there is very little water. Cacti are an example. They grow in desert climates.

Many plants cannot survive very cold temperatures. Live oak trees, for example, may be killed by frost. Orange trees need both rainfall and warm temperatures to grow well.

▶ **2** **DEFINE:** What is vegetation?

Climate and Animals
Animals that eat certain plants can live only in climates where those plants grow. For example, eucalyptus leaves are the main food of koalas. Koalas live only in areas where eucalyptus trees can grow.

▲ **Figure 5-16** Koalas eat mainly eucalyptus leaves.

Figure 5-15 ▶
Major land biomes found on Earth

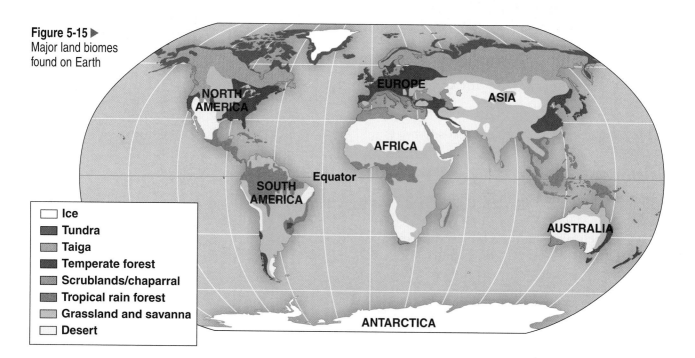

NORTH AMERICA
EUROPE
ASIA
AFRICA
Equator
SOUTH AMERICA
AUSTRALIA
ANTARCTICA

- ☐ Ice
- ☐ Tundra
- ☐ Taiga
- ☐ Temperate forest
- ☐ Scrublands/chaparral
- ☐ Tropical rain forest
- ☐ Grassland and savanna
- ☐ Desert

Other animals are directly affected by temperature. The body temperature of cold-blooded animals is about the same as the air temperature. The animals would die if the air temperature was too low. Most snakes, for example, live in warm climates. They could not survive in a cold climate.

 NAME: What are two ways animals are affected by climate?

✓ CHECKING CONCEPTS

1. What is a biome?
2. How are scientists able to identify different biomes?
3. What are all the plants in a biome called?
4. What are two climate factors that can affect vegetation?
5. What kind of climate do most species of snakes live in?

THINKING CRITICALLY

6. **INFER:** Giant pandas are raccoonlike animals. They eat only bamboo shoots. Bamboo grows only in China and Tibet. Where do you think giant pandas live? Explain.
7. **HYPOTHESIZE:** There is a forest biome in the northern United States that is called the spruce-moose belt. How might this area have received this name?

INTERPRETING VISUALS

Use Figure 5-15 to answer the following questions.

8. **IDENTIFY:** Which type of biome covers the most land area?
9. **ANALYZE:** Which type of biome has hot and wet weather?
10. **INFER:** Which type of biome has hot and dry weather?

 ## *Integrating Environmental Science*

TOPICS: natural resources, ecosystems

TROPICAL RAIN FORESTS

Tropical rain forests are very dense areas of vegetation. They have hot, humid climates. Many different kinds of animals and plants live in rain forests. Scientists estimate that in 10 square km, there may be more than 750 different species of trees and more than 1,000 different species of animals.

Many rain-forest plants are natural resources for medicines and other products. Some rain-forest animals are found nowhere else. Scientists are concerned because the rain forests are being cut down, burned, and used for farming and development. Once the nutrients in the soil are gone, farmers move to a new area. Many countries are trying to stop the destruction of the rain forests. They also hope to save some species that are in danger of extinction.

Thinking Critically What are some ways governments can help stop the rain forests from being destroyed?

▲ **Figure 5-17** Tropical orchids produce the flavoring of vanilla from vanilla beans. The beans (right) are found in rain forests from Florida to South America.

THE Big IDEA

How do organisms adapt to climate?

In nature, you would never see a palm tree and a cactus plant growing in the same location. Each type of plant is suited to a particular climate. A palm tree grows best in a warm, moist, tropical climate. A cactus grows best in a hot, dry, desert climate. A palm tree could not survive in the Arctic. A cactus could not survive in a tropical location.

Most living things have adaptations that help them survive in their climate zone. Adaptations are features that let an organism live and reproduce in its environment.

Look at the map and photographs that appear on these two pages. Then, follow the directions in the Science Log to learn more about "the big idea."✦

Bighorn Sheep
Bighorns are wild sheep found only in North America. Their feet are adapted to gripping slippery surfaces. This helps them leap across mountain ledges.

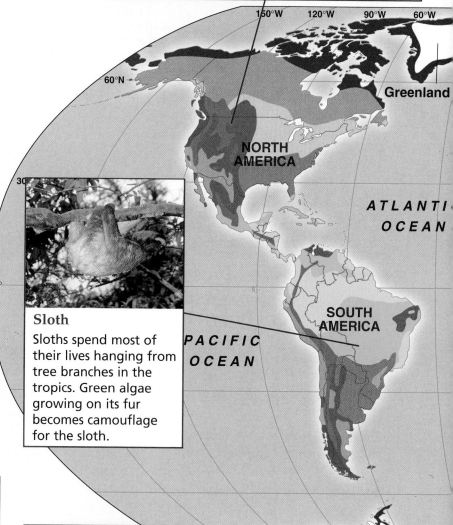

Sloth
Sloths spend most of their lives hanging from tree branches in the tropics. Green algae growing on its fur becomes camouflage for the sloth.

TROPICAL RAINY	TEMPERATE
☐ Tropical wet	CONTINENTAL
☐ Tropical wet-and-dry	☐ Humid continental
DRY	☐ Subarctic
☐ Semiarid	**POLAR**
☐ Arid	☐ Tundra
TEMPERATE MARINE	☐ Ice cap
☐ Mediterranean	**HIGHLANDS**
☐ Humid subtropical	☐ Highlands
☐ Marine west coast	

Penguin
Unlike other birds, penguins cannot fly. Their winglike flippers are well suited to their watery life. Thick layers of body fat help them survive in the cold polar regions.

▲ **Figure 5-18**
Each type of living thing has adaptations suited for life in its particular climate zone.

Polar Bear

Polar bears have light-colored fur that blends into the snow. Their heavy fur coats and layers of body fat keep the animals warm in frigid waters.

Arctic Lichen

Arctic lichens are fungi that partner with algae. Because lichens lack roots, they can survive the cycle of thawing and freezing that occurs in the permanently frozen ground that covers the Arctic.

Giant Rafflesia

Rain forests are home to the largest flowers in the world, the Giant Rafflesias. The plants that produce these huge flowers lack leaves and stems. They smell like rotting meat to attract the flies that pollinate them.

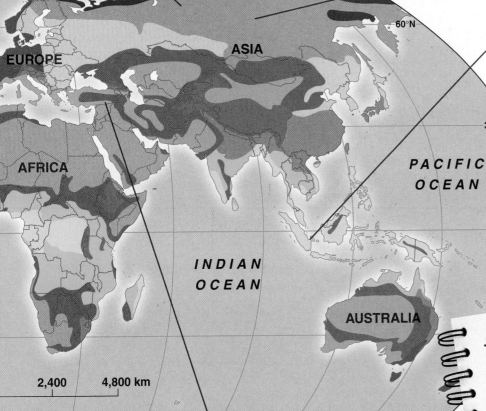

0°   30°E   60°E   90°E   120°E   150

60°N

ASIA

EUROPE

30°N

AFRICA

PACIFIC OCEAN

0°

INDIAN OCEAN

AUSTRALIA

60°S

0   2,400   4,800 km

ANTARCTICA

Camel

Camels have long eyelashes that protect their eyes from blowing sand. Thick eyebrows shade their eyes from the harsh Sun. The hump is a pad of fat used for energy when food is scarce. Because it does not sweat much, a camel can hold a lot of water in its body.

Science Log

WRITING ACTIVITY

The tundra covers about one-fifth of Earth's land surface. To survive its freezing temperatures, organisms must have special adaptations. Find out what animals live in the tundra. Pick one and write an essay explaining how it can survive in this harsh environment. Start your search at www.conceptsandchallenges.com.

Chapter Summary

Lesson 5-1

- **Climate** is the average weather conditions in an area from year to year. Average monthly and yearly temperature, temperature range, and average precipitation are used to describe climate.

Lesson 5-2

- An area's climate is affected by its **latitude** and **altitude.**
- Ocean currents affect the temperatures of areas along coasts.
- The leeward sides of mountains have warmer, drier climates than the windward sides of mountains do.

Lesson 5-3

- A climate zone is an area with a given yearly temperature range and regular weather patterns. The three climate zones are the **tropical zone,** the **polar zone,** and the **middle-latitude zone.**
- The climates in each climate zone can be characterized by temperature and amount of rainfall.

Lesson 5-4

- Local climates are formed by local conditions. Very small climate zones are called **microclimates.** Cities are microclimates.
- Human activities and skyscrapers can affect the climate in an area. Global warming due to increased air pollution could cause temperatures to rise around the world.

Lesson 5-5

- A **biome** is a large region of Earth that has a characteristic climate and certain kinds of living things. It is characterized by the plant life found there.
- Climate affects the **vegetation** in an area.
- The animals and other organisms in an area are affected by climate.

Key Term Challenges

altitude (p. 118)
biome (p. 126)
climate (p. 116)
latitude (p. 118)
microclimate (p. 122)
middle-latitude zone (p. 120)
polar zone (p. 120)
tropical zone (p. 120)
vegetation (p. 126)
weather (p. 116)

MATCHING Write the Key Term from above that best matches each description.

1. warm region near the equator
2. large region with a characteristic climate and plant and animal communities
3. average weather conditions in an area from year to year
4. cold region near the poles
5. height above sea level
6. day to day conditions of the atmosphere
7. distance north or south of the equator in degrees
8. region between 30° and 60°N and S latitudes
9. plants
10. very small climate zone

IDENTIFYING WORD RELATIONSHIPS Explain how the words in each pair are related. Write your answers in complete sentences.

11. altitude, latitude
12. biome, vegetation
13. climate, weather
14. microclimate, local climate
15. tropical zone, middle-latitude zone

Content Challenges TEST PREP

FILL IN Write the term or phrase that best completes each statement.

1. To find average temperature, you add two or more temperatures and divide the sum by the number of _____.

2. The amount of temperature change in an area is its temperature _____.

3. Rain, snow, sleet, and hail are forms of _____.

4. At higher latitudes, the Sun's rays strike Earth _____.

5. Areas at low latitudes have a _____ climate than areas at higher latitudes do.

6. Air is _____ at sea level than it is at higher altitudes.

7. Land areas near cold-water currents have _____ temperatures than land areas near warm-water currents do.

8. When air passes over a mountain range, it rises and _____.

9. It hardly ever rains on the _____ side of a mountain.

10. The leeward side of a mountain is the side of the mountain that faces _____ the wind.

11. The tropical zone is located between _____ north and south latitude.

12. Some scientists think that _____ will lead to global warming.

13. Energy from the _____ is the biggest factor influencing weather and climate.

14. Biomes are identified mainly by the type of _____ found in the area.

15. The type of vegetation found in an area depends on the area's _____.

TRUE/FALSE Write *true* if the statement is true. If the statement is false, change the underlined term to make the statement true.

16. The day-to-day condition of the atmosphere is called the climate.

17. The leeward side of a mountain gets more rain than the windward side.

18. Dry climates are also described as arid.

19. Antarctica is located in the tropical zone.

20. A city is an example of a microclimate.

21. Latitude, ocean currents, and mountains affect an area's climate.

22. Climate has never changed during Earth's history.

23. Each biome has certain kinds of plants and animals.

24. Most snakes live in cool climates.

25. Cacti grow best in tundra climates.

26. Average daily temperature and temperature range are both used to describe the climate of an area.

27. The temperature gets colder as you climb a mountain.

28. Global warming might cause sea levels to fall.

29. A rain shadow is sometimes found on the windward side of a mountain.

30. The tilt of Earth directly influences climate and weather.

Concept Challenges TEST PREP

WRITTEN RESPONSE **Answer the following questions in complete sentences.**

1. **PREDICT:** What kind of climate would a coastal town located near a cold-water current have?

2. **INFER:** Why are many deserts located on the leeward sides of mountains?

3. **INFER:** If Earth had no tilt, how would this affect the world's climates?

4. **EXPLAIN:** How do the types of objects found in a city help to create a microclimate?

5. **INFER:** Why would vegetation affect the types of animals that can live in a biome?

6. **INFER:** Why is having a stem that stores water an important adaptation for a cactus?

INTERPRETING VISUALS **Use Figure 5-19 below to answer the following questions.**

7. Which biome is found most often along the equator?

8. Which biome covers most of Australia?

9. What are the biomes found in North America?

10. Where is polar ice found? Why?

11. Which continent has the most biomes? What are they?

12. Which biome do you live in? What are some common plants and animals that are found in this biome?

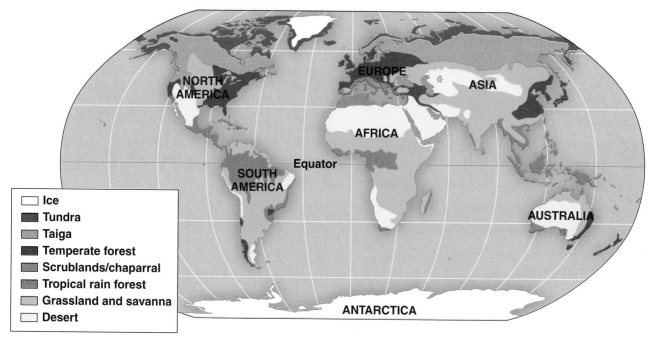

▲ Figure 5-19

Appendix A Metric System

The Metric System and SI Units

The metric system is an international system of measurement based on units of ten. More than 90% of the nations of the world use the metric system. In the United States, both the English system and the metric system are used.

The *Système International*, or SI, has been used as the international measurement system since 1960. The SI is a modernized version of the metric system. Like the metric system, the SI is a decimal system based on units of ten. When you want to change from one unit in the metric system to another unit, you multiply or divide by a multiple of ten.

- When you change from a smaller unit to a larger unit, you divide.

- When you change from a larger unit to a smaller unit, you multiply.

COMMON METRIC PREFIXES			
micro-	0.000001 or 1/1,000,000	deka-	10
milli-	0.001 or 1/1,000	hecto-	100
centi-	0.01 or 1/100	kilo-	1,000
deci-	0.1 or 1/10	mega-	1,000,000

▲ Figure 2

METRIC UNITS		
LENGTH	SYMBOL	RELATIONSHIP
kilometer	km	1 km = 1,000 m
meter	m	1 m = 100 cm
centimeter	cm	1 cm = 10 mm
millimeter	mm	1 mm = 0.1 cm
AREA	SYMBOL	
square kilometer	km^2	$1\ km^2 = 1,000,000\ m^2$
square meter	m^2	$1\ m^2 = 1,000,000\ mm^2$
square centimeter	cm^2	$1\ cm^2 = 0.0001\ m^2$
square millimeter	mm^2	$1\ mm^2 = 0.000001\ m^2$
VOLUME	SYMBOL	
cubic meter	m^3	$1\ m^3 = 1,000,000\ cm^3$
cubic centimeter	cm^3	$1\ cm^3 = 0.000001\ m^3$
liter	L	1 L = 1,000 mL
milliliter	mL	1 mL = 0.001 L
MASS	SYMBOL	
metric ton	t	1 t = 1,000 kg
kilogram	kg	1 kg = 1,000 g
gram	g	1 g = 1,000 mg
centigram	cg	1 cg = 10 mg
milligram	mg	1 mg = 0.001 g
TEMPERATURE	SYMBOL	
Kelvin	K	
degree Celsius	°C	

▲ Figure 1

METRIC-STANDARD EQUIVALENTS	
SI to English	English to SI
LENGTH	
1 kilometer = 0.621 mile (mi)	1 mi = 1.61 km
1 meter = 1.094 yards (yd)	1 yd = 0.914 m
1 meter = 3.28 feet (ft)	1 ft = 0.305 m
1 centimeter = 0.394 inch (in.)	1 in. = 2.54 cm
1 millimeter = 0.039 inch	1 in. = 25.4 mm
AREA	
1 square kilometer = 0.3861 square mile	$1\ mi^2 = 2.590\ km^2$
1 square meter = 1.1960 square yards	$1\ yd^2 = 0.8361\ m^2$
1 square meter = 10.763 square feet	$1\ ft^2 = 0.0929\ m^2$
1 square centimeter = 0.155 square inch	$1\ in.^2 = 6.452\ cm^2$
VOLUME	
1 cubic meter = 1.3080 cubic yards	$1\ yd^3 = 0.7646\ m^3$
1 cubic meter = 35.315 cubic feet	$1\ ft^3 = 0.0283\ m^3$
1 cubic centimeter = 0.0610 cubic inch	$1\ in.^3 = 16.39\ cm^3$
1 liter = 0.2642 gallon (gal)	1 gal = 3.79 L
1 liter = 1.06 quarts (qt)	1 qt = 0.946 L
1 liter = 2.11 pints (pt)	1 pt = 0.47 L
1 milliliter = 0.034 fluid ounce (fl oz)	1 fl oz = 29.57 mL
MASS	
1 metric ton = 0.984 ton	1 ton = 1.016 t
1 kilogram = 2.205 pounds (lb)	1 lb = 0.4536 kg
1 gram = 0.0353 ounce (oz)	1 oz = 28.35 g
TEMPERATURE	
Celsius = 5/9(°F − 32)	Fahrenheit = 9/5°C + 32
0°C = 32°F (Freezing point of water)	72°F = 22°C (Room temperature)
100°C = 212°F (Boiling point of water)	98.6°F = 37°C (Human body temperature)
Kelvin = (°F + 459.67)/1.8	Fahrenheit = (K × 1.8) − 459.67

▲ Figure 3

Appendix B Chemical Elements

LIST OF CHEMICAL ELEMENTS

Element	Atomic Symbol	Atomic Number
Actinium	Ac	89
Aluminum	Al	13
Americium	Am	95
Antimony	Sb	51
Argon	Ar	18
Arsenic	As	33
Astatine	At	85
Barium	Ba	56
Berkelium	Bk	97
Beryllium	Be	4
Bismuth	Bi	83
Bohrium	Bh	107
Boron	B	5
Bromine	Br	35
Cadmium	Cd	48
Calcium	Ca	20
Californium	Cf	98
Carbon	C	6
Cerium	Ce	58
Cesium	Cs	55
Chlorine	Cl	17
Chromium	Cr	24
Cobalt	Co	27
Copper	Cu	29
Curium	Cm	96
Dubnium	Db	105
Dysprosium	Dy	66
Einsteinium	Es	99
Erbium	Er	68
Europium	Eu	63
Fermium	Fm	100
Fluorine	F	9
Francium	Fr	87
Gadolinium	Gd	64
Gallium	Ga	31
Germanium	Ge	32
Gold	Au	79

▲ Figure 4

LIST OF CHEMICAL ELEMENTS

Element	Atomic Symbol	Atomic Number
Hafnium	Hf	72
Hassium	Hs	108
Helium	He	2
Holmium	Ho	67
Hydrogen	H	1
Indium	In	49
Iodine	I	53
Iridium	Ir	77
Iron	Fe	26
Krypton	Kr	36
Lanthanum	La	57
Lawrencium	Lr	103
Lead	Pb	82
Lithium	Li	3
Lutetium	Lu	71
Magnesium	Mg	12
Manganese	Mn	25
Meitnerium	Mt	109
Mendelevium	Md	101
Mercury	Hg	80
Molybdenum	Mo	42
Neodymium	Nd	60
Neon	Ne	10
Neptunium	Np	93
Nickel	Ni	28
Niobium	Nb	41
Nitrogen	N	7
Nobelium	No	102
Osmium	Os	76
Oxygen	O	8
Palladium	Pd	46
Phosphorus	P	15
Platinum	Pt	78
Plutonium	Pu	94
Polonium	Po	84
Potassium	K	19
Praseodymium	Pr	59
Promethium	Pm	61

LIST OF CHEMICAL ELEMENTS

Element	Atomic Symbol	Atomic Number
Protactinium	Pa	91
Radium	Ra	88
Radon	Rn	86
Rhenium	Re	75
Rhodium	Rh	45
Rubidium	Rb	37
Ruthenium	Ru	44
Rutherfordium	Rf	104
Samarium	Sm	62
Scandium	Sc	21
Seaborgium	Sg	106
Selenium	Se	34
Silicon	Si	14
Silver	Ag	47
Sodium	Na	11
Strontium	Sr	38
Sulfur	S	16
Tantalum	Ta	73
Technetium	Tc	43
Tellurium	Te	52
Terbium	Tb	65
Thallium	Tl	81
Thorium	Th	90
Thulium	Tm	69
Tin	Sn	50
Titanium	Ti	22
Tungsten	W	74
Ununnilium	Uun	110
Unununium	Uuu	111
Ununbium	Uub	112
Ununquadium	Uuq	114
Uranium	U	92
Vanadium	V	23
Xenon	Xe	54
Ytterbium	Yb	70
Yttrium	Y	39
Zinc	Zn	30
Zirconium	Zr	40

Appendix C Science Terms

Analyzing Science Terms

You can often unlock the meaning of an unfamiliar science term by analyzing its word parts. Prefixes and suffixes, for example, each carry a meaning that comes from a word root. This word root usually comes from the Latin or Greek language. The following list of prefixes and suffixes provides clues to the meaning of many science terms.

WORD PART	MEANING	EXAMPLE
astr-, aster-	star	astronomy
bar-, baro-	weight, pressure	barometer
batho-, bathy-	depth	batholith, bathysphere
circum-	around	circum-Pacific, circumpolar
-cline	lean, slope	anticline, syncline
eco-	environment	ecology, ecosystem
epi-	on	epicenter
ex-, exo-	out, outside of	exosphere, exfoliation, extrusion
geo-	earth	geode, geology, geomagnetic
-graph	write, writing	seismograph
hydro-	water	hydrosphere
hypo-	under	hypothesis
iso-	equal	isoscope, isostasy, isotope
-lith, -lithic	stone	Neolithic, regolith
magn-	great, large	magnitude
mar-	sea	marine
meso-	middle	mesosphere, Mesozoic
meta-	among, change	metamorphic, metamorphism
micro-	small	microquake
-morph, -morphic	form	metamorphic
neo-	new	Neolithic
paleo-	old	paleontology, Paleozoic
ped-, pedo-	ground, soil	pediment
peri-	around	perigee, perihelion
-ose	carbohydrate	glucose, cellulose
seism-, seismo-	shake, earthquake	seismic, seismograph
sol-	sun	solar, solstice
spectro-	look at, examine	spectroscope, spectrum
-sphere	ball, globe	hemisphere, lithosphere
strati-, strato-	spread, layer	stratification, stratovolcano
terra-	earth, land	terracing, terrane
thermo-	heat	thermosphere
top-, topo-	place	topographic
tropo-	turn, respond to	tropopause, troposphere

▲ Figure 5

Appendix **D** Meteorological Scales

Saffir-Simpson Hurricane Scale

The Saffir-Simpson scale measures the wind speed of hurricanes. The category number tells the wind speed and amount of damage a hurricane can cause. Since the 1970s, the National Hurricane Center in the United States has used this scale to classify hurricanes. The scale was developed by Herbert Saffir, an engineer, and Robert Simpson, a former director of the National Hurricane Center. The National Hurricane Center is located on the campus of Florida International University, Miami, Florida. The Center is part of NOAA, the National Oceanic and Atmospheric Administration.

CATEGORY	WIND SPEED (mph)	DAMAGE
1	74–95	Minor
2	96–110	Moderate
3	111–130	Strong
4	131–155	Very Strong
5	More than 155	Devastating

◀ Figure 6

Beaufort Wind Speed Scale

This scale is named for the nineteenth-century British naval officer who devised it. The Beaufort Scale classifies wind speed according to its effects. It was originally used in 1806 as an aid for sailors. It has since been adapted for use on land. The scale has been modified through the years.

CODE	SPEED (MPH)	DESCRIPTION	EFFECTS ON LAND
0	Below 1	Calm	Smoke rises vertically
1	1–5	Light air	Smoke drifts slowly
2	6–11	Light breeze	Leaves rustle
3	12–19	Gentle breeze	Leaves and twigs move
4	20–29	Moderate breeze	Small branches move
5	30–39	Fresh breeze	Small trees sway
6	40–50	Strong breeze	Large branches sway
7	51–61	Near gale	Walking difficult
8	62–74	Gale	Twigs snap off trees
9	75–87	Strong gale	Minor damage
10	88–101	Whole gale	Significant damage
11	102–117	Storm	Widespread damage
12	Above 118	Hurricane	Widespread destruction

◀ Figure 7

The Fujita Intensity Scale

This scale provides a measure of the strength of a tornado. It was developed by tornado specialist Dr. Tetsuto Theodore Fujita, of the University of Chicago.

CATEGORY	WIND SPEED (mph)	DAMAGE
F0	40–71	Light
F1	72–112	Moderate
F2	113–157	Considerable
F3	158–206	Severe
F4	207–260	Devastating
F5	261–318	Incredible

◀ Figure 8

Appendix **E**   Mathematics Review

Multiplying Integers

When you multiply integers, you must decide if the answer is positive or negative.

If the signs of the integers are the same, the product is positive.

$$+5 \times +4 = +20$$
$$-5 \times -4 = +20$$

If the signs of the integers are different, the product is negative.

$$+5 \times -4 = -20$$
$$-5 \times +4 = -20$$

Dividing Integers

The rules for dividing integers are the same as the rules for multiplying integers.

If the signs of the integers are the same, the quotient is positive.

$$-36 \div -9 = +4$$
$$+36 \div +9 = +4$$

If the signs of the integers are different, the quotient is negative.

$$-36 \div +9 = -4$$
$$+36 \div -9 = -4$$

Solving an Equation

To solve an equation, find the value of the variable that makes the equation true.

Is $b = 3$ the solution to the equation?

$$4b = 12$$

Replace b with 3 in the equation.

$$4 \times 3 = 12$$
$$12 = 12$$

Yes, $b = 3$ is the solution to the equation.

Changing a Decimal to a Percent

To change a decimal to a percent, multiply the decimal by 100%.

> Find the efficiency of a machine if the work output is 5 J and the work input is 10 J.
>
> Efficiency = work output ÷ work input × 100%
>
> Efficiency = 5 J ÷ 10 J × 100%
>
> Efficiency = 0.5 × 100%
>
> Efficiency = 50%
>
> Notice that when you multiply 0.5 by 100%, the decimal point moves two places to the right.

Solving Word Problems

To solve distance problems, you can use $d = r \times t$ or $d = rt$.

> The Smiths drove 220 miles at an average speed of 55 miles per hour. How long did the trip take?

PLAN

> Substitute the values you know into the equation $d = r \times t$.
>
> Then solve.

DO

$$220 = 55t$$
$$220 \div 55 = 55t \div 55$$
$$4 = t$$

SOLUTION

The trip took 4 hours.

Glossary

Pronunciation and syllabication have been derived from *Webster's New World Dictionary*, Second College Edition, Revised School Printing (Prentice Hall, 1985). Syllables printed in capital letters are given primary stress. (Numbers in parentheses indicate the page number, or page numbers, on which the term is defined.)

	PRONUNCIATION KEY				
Symbol	Example	Respelling	Symbol	Example	Respelling
a	transpiration	(tran-spuh-RAY-shuhn)	oh	biome	(BY-ohm)
ah	composite	(kuhm-PAHZ-iht)	oi	asteroid	(AS-tuhr-oid)
aw	atoll	(A-tawl)	oo	altitude	(AL-tuh-tood)
ay	abrasion	(uh-BRAY-zhuhn)	ow	compound	(KAHM-pownd)
ch	leaching	(LEECH-ing)	s	satellite	(SAT-uhl-yt)
eh	chemical	(KEHM-i-kuhl)	sh	specialization	(spehsh-uhl-ih-ZAY-shuhn)
ee	equinox	(EE-kwih-nahks)	th	thermocline	(THUR-muh-klyn)
f	hemisphere	(HEHM-ih-sfeer)	th	weathering	(WEHTH-uhr-ing)
g	galaxy	(GAL-uhk-see)	uh	volcanism	(VAHL-kuh-nihzm)
ih	anticline	(AN-tih-klyn)	y, eye	anticline, isobar	(AN-tih-klyn), (EYE-soh-bahr)
j	geologic	(jee-uh-LAHJ-ihk)	yoo	cumulus	(KYOOM-yuh-luhs)
k	current	(KUR-uhnt)	z	deposition	(dehp-uh-ZIHSH-uhn)
ks	axis	(AK-sihs)	zh	erosion	(e-ROH-zhuhn)

adaptations (ad-uhp-TAY-shuhnz): features of an organism that let it live and reproduce in its environment (p. 128)

air current: up-and-down movement of air (p. 74)

air mass: large volume of air with about the same temperature and amount of moisture throughout (p. 100)

altitude (AL-tuh-tood): height above sea level (p. 118)

anemometer (an-uh-MAHM-uht-uhr): instrument that measures wind speed (p. 80)

atmosphere (AT-muhs-feer): envelope of gases that surrounds Earth (p. 60)

atoll (A-tawl): ring-shaped coral reef around a lagoon (p. 52)

barometer (buh-RAHM-uht-uhr): instrument used to measure air pressure (p. 70)

barrier reef: coral reef that forms around a sunken volcanic island (p. 52)

bathysphere (BATH-uh-sfeer): one of the first underwater research vessels (p. 36)

benthos: organisms that live on the ocean floor (p. 54)

biome (BY-ohm): large region with a characteristic climate and plant and animal communities (p. 126)

capacity (kuh-PAS-ih-tee): amount of material something can hold (p. 88)

cellular respiration (rehs-puh-RAY-shuhn): process by which a cell releases energy from food molecules (p. 60)

cirrus (SIR-uhs) **cloud:** light, feathery cloud (p. 94)

climate (KLY-muht): average weather conditions of an area over many years (p. 116)

cold front: forward edge of a cold air mass, formed when a cold air mass pushes under a warm air mass (p. 102)

communication: sharing information (p. 8)

condensation (kahn-duhn-SAY-shuhn): changing of a gas to a liquid (pp. 16, 92)

conduction (kuhn-DUHK-shuhn): transfer of heat through matter by direct contact (p. 66)

constant: something that does not change (p. 11)

continental shelf: part of a continent that slopes gently away from the shoreline (p. 50)

continental slope: part of a continent between the continental shelf and the ocean floor (p. 50)

controlled experiment: experiment in which all the conditions except one are kept constant (p. 11)

convection: process by which heat is transferred through a liquid or a gas (p. 66)

coral: small animals found in warm, shallow ocean waters (p. 52)

Coriolis effect: bending of Earth's winds and ocean currents by Earth's rotation (p. 40)

crest: highest point of a wave (p. 42)

cumulus (KYOO-myuh-luhs) **cloud:** big, puffy cloud (p. 94)

current: stream of water flowing in the oceans (p. 40)

data: information you collect when you observe something (p. 3)

density current: stream of water that moves up and down in ocean depths (p. 40)

dew point: temperature to which air must be cooled to reach saturation (p. 92)

ebb tide: outgoing or falling tide (p. 46)

evaporation (ee-vap-uh-RAY-shuhn): changing of a liquid to a gas (pp. 16, 86)

flood tide: incoming or rising tide (p. 46)

fringing reef: coral reef that is directly attached to a shore (p. 52)

front: boundary between air masses of different densities (p. 102)

frost: ice formed from condensation below the freezing point of water (p. 92)

geyser (GY-zuhr): heated groundwater that erupts onto Earth's surface (p. 20)

global winds: large systems of winds around Earth (p. 76)

gram: basic unit of mass (p. 4)

groundwater: water that collects in pores in soil and sinks into the ground (p. 18)

guyot (GEE-oh): flat-topped, underwater seamount (p. 50)

humidity: amount of water vapor in the air (p. 88)

hurricane (HUR-ih-kayn): tropical storm with very strong winds (p. 104)

hypothesis: suggested answer to a question or problem (p. 10)

ionosphere (eye-AHN-uh-sfeer): upper layer of the atmosphere (p. 62)

isobar (EYE-soh-bahr): line on a weather map that connects points of equal air pressure (p. 110)

isotherm: line on a weather map that joins places that have the same temperatures (p. 110)

kettle lake: lake formed by a retreating glacier (p. 26)

lagoon: shallow body of water between a reef and the mainland (p. 52)

lake: low spot in Earth's surface filled with still water (p. 26)

latitude (LAT-uh-tood): distance north or south of the equator in degrees (p. 118)

liter: basic unit of liquid volume (p. 4)

mass: amount of matter in something (p. 4)

matter: anything that has mass and volume (p. 60)

meander (mee-AN-duhr): loop in a mature river (p. 22)

meniscus: curve at the surface of a liquid in a thin tube (p. 4)

mesosphere (MEHZ-uh-sfeer): third layer of the atmosphere (p. 62)

meter: basic unit of length or distance (p. 4)

microclimate (MY-kroh-kly-muht): very small climate zone (p. 122)

middle-latitude zone: region between 30° and 60° N and S latitude (p. 120)

millibar (MIHL-ih-bahr): unit of measurement for air pressure (p. 108)

model: tool scientists use to represent an object or a process (p. 3)

monsoon: wind that changes direction with the seasons (p. 78)

nekton (NEK-tahn): free-swimming ocean animals (p. 54)

newton: metric unit of force (p. 68)

nodule (NAHJ-ool): mineral lump found on the ocean floor (p. 48)

oceanography (oh-shuh-NAHG-ruh-fee): study of Earth's oceans (p. 34)

ooze: ocean sediment that contains the remains of many ocean organisms (p. 48)

oxbow lake: curved lake formed when a bend in a river is cut off at both ends (p. 22)

phytoplankton (fyt-oh-PLANK-tuhn): source of food for floating animals in the ocean (p. 54)

plankton (PLANK-tuhn): floating organisms in the ocean (p. 54)

polar air mass: air mass that forms over cold regions (p. 100)

polar zone: cold region above 60° N and below 60° S latitude (p. 120)

pond: body of water similar to a lake but usually smaller and shallower (p. 26)

pore: tiny hole or space (p. 18)

potable (POHT-uh-buhl): water that is fit to drink (p. 39)

precipitation (pree-sihp-uh-TAY-shuhn): water that falls to Earth's surface from the atmosphere (pp. 16, 98)

pressure: amount of force per unit of area (p. 68)

psychrometer (sy-KRAHM-uht-uhr): instrument used to find relative humidity (p. 50)

radiant (RAY-dee-uhnt) **energy:** energy given off by the Sun that can travel through empty space (p. 64)

radiation (ray-dee-AY-shuhn): movement of the Sun's energy through empty space (p. 64)

rain gauge (GAYJ): device used to measure precipitation (p. 98)

rapids: part of a river where the current is swift (p. 22)

relative humidity: amount of water vapor in the air compared with the amount of water vapor the air can hold at capacity (p. 90)

reservoir: artificial lake (p. 26)

salinity (suh-LIHN-uh-tee): amount of dissolved salts in ocean water (p. 38)

saturated (sach-uh-RAYT-ihd): filled to capacity (p. 88)

seamount: volcanic mountain on the ocean floor (p. 50)

simulation: computer model that usually shows a process (p. 3)

sling psychrometer (sy-KRAHM-uht-uhr): instrument used to find relative humidity (p. 90)

sonar: system that bounces sound waves off the ocean floor (p. 36)

specific humidity (hyoo-MIHD-uh-tee): actual amount of water in the air (p. 88)

spring: natural flow of groundwater to Earth's surface (p. 20)

station model: record of weather information at a weather station (p. 108)

stratosphere (STRAT-uh-sfeer): second layer of the atmosphere (p. 62)

stratus (STRAT-uhs) **cloud:** sheetlike cloud that forms layers across the sky (p. 94)

submersible (suhb-MUHR-suh-buhl): underwater research vessel (p. 36)

temperature: measurement of the amount of heat energy something contains (p. 4)

theory: set of hypotheses that have been supported by testing over and over again (p. 10)

thermocline (THUR-muh-klyn): layer of ocean water in which the temperature drops sharply with depth (p. 38)

thermosphere (THUR-muh-sfeer): upper layer of the ionosphere (p. 62)

thunderstorm: storm with thunder, lightning, and often heavy rain and strong winds (p. 104)

tide: regular change in the level of Earth's oceans (p. 46)

tornado (tawr-NAY-doh): small, very violent, funnel-shaped cloud that spins (p. 104)

transpiration (trans-spuh-RAY-shuhn): process by which plants give off water vapor into the air (p. 86)

trench: deep canyon on the ocean floor (p. 50)

tropical (TRAHP-ih-kuhl) **air mass:** air mass that forms over warm regions (p. 100)

tropical (TRAHP-ih-kuhl) **zone:** warm region near the equator (p. 120)

troposphere (TROH-puh-sfeer): lowest layer of the atmosphere (p. 62)

trough (TRAWF): lowest point of a wave (p. 42)

unit: amount used to measure something (p. 4)

variable: anything that can affect the outcome of an experiment (p. 11)

vegetation (vej-uh-TAY-shuhn): plants (p. 126)

volume: amount of space an object takes up (p. 4)

warm front: forward edge of a warm air mass, formed when a warm air mass pushes over a cold air mass (p. 102)

water cycle: repeated pattern of water movement between Earth and the atmosphere (p. 16)

waterfall: steep fall of water, as of a stream, from a height (p. 22)

water table: upper layer of saturated rock and soil (p. 18)

wave: regular up-and-down movement of water (p. 42)

weather: day-to-day conditions of the atmosphere (p. 116)

well: hole dug below the water table that fills with groundwater (p. 20)

wind: horizontal movement of air (p. 74)

wind vane: instrument that indicates wind direction (p. 80)

world ocean: body of salt water covering much of Earth's surface (p. 34)

Index

Photo Credits

Photography Credits: All photographs are by the Pearson Learning Group (PLG), John Serafin for PLG, and David Mager for PLG, except as noted below.

Cover: *bkgd.* Simon Fraser/Science Photo Library/Photo Researchers, Inc.; *inset* Rod Planck/Photo Researchers, Inc.

Table of Contents: v t Barbara K. Hesse/Visuals Unlimited, Inc.; v b NASA/Goddard Space Flight Center/Science Photo Library/Photo Researchers, Inc.

Frontmatter: P001 bl Science VU/Visuals Unlimited, Inc.; P001 mr George Ranalli/Photo Researchers, Inc.; P001 tr Farrell Grehan/Photo Researchers, Inc.; P001 Comstock, Inc.; P002 bl Jane Grushow/Grant Heilman Photography, Inc.; P002 br Eric Kamp/Phototake; P002 tr AFP/Corbis; P003 Comstock, Inc.; P005 Pearson Learning; P005 r Comstock, Inc.; P007 r Comstock, Inc.; P009 br Bob Daemmrich/Stock, Boston, Inc.; P009 mr USDA/Natural Resources Conservation Service; P009 tr SuperStock, Inc; P009 r Comstock, Inc.; P010 Frans Lanting/Minden Pictures; P011 r Comstock, Inc.; P013 r Comstock, Inc.

Chapter 1: P15 Clyde H. Smith/Peter Arnold, Inc.; P19 Stephen L. Alvarez/National Geographic Society; P20 Brian Yarvin/Photo Researchers, Inc.; P21 E. R. Degginger/Color-Pic, Inc.; P22 Murray Wilson/Omni-Photo Communications; P23 James Sheffer/Photoedit; P27 b Worldsat International, Inc./Photo Researchers, Inc.; P27 t Carr Clifton/Minden Pictures; P30 Clyde H. Smith/Peter Arnold, Inc.; P31 Clyde H. Smith/Peter Arnold, Inc.; P32 Clyde H. Smith/Peter Arnold, Inc.

Chapter 2: P33 Australian Picture Library/Corbis; P34 David B. Fleetham/Visuals Unlimited, Inc.; P35 Douglas Faulkner/The Stock Market; P37 b Patricia Jordan/Peter Arnold, Inc.; P37 t Stuart Westmorland/Photo Researchers, Inc.; P39 Yann Arthus-Bertrand/Corbis; P46 b Jim Brandenburg/Minden Pictures; P46 t Jim Brandenburg/Minden Pictures; P47 Tom McHugh/Photo Researchers, Inc.; P48 bl Jim Steinberg/Photo Researchers, Inc.; P48 br Jan Hinsch/Science Photo Library/Photo Researchers, Inc.; P48 tr Charles D. Winters/Photo Researchers, Inc.; P51 Pavlovsky/Photo Researchers, Inc.; P52 l David Hall/Photo Researchers, Inc.; P52 r Jean-Marc Truchet/Getty Images; P53 b Steve Wolper/DRK Photo; P53 t Douglas Faulkner/Photo Researchers, Inc.; P54 b David Wrobel/Visuals Unlimited; P54 t Jan Hinsch/Science Photo Library/Photo Researchers, Inc.; P55 Thomas Kitchin/Tom Stack & Associates; P56 Australian Picture Library/Corbis; P57 Australian Picture Library/Corbis; P58 Australian Picture Library/Corbis

Chapter 3: P59 Barbara K. Hesse/Visuals Unlimited, Inc.; P61 Dennis Kunkel/MicroVision; P63 Michael Giannechini/Photo Researchers, Inc.; P65 David DuCros/Science Photo Library/Photo Researchers, Inc.; P67 Barbara K. Hesse/Visuals Unlimited, Inc.; P70 l Bruce Heinemann/PhotoDisc, Inc.; P70 m Yoav Levy/Phototake; P70 r Leonard Lessin/Peter Arnold, Inc.; P71 b The Granger Collection; P71 t Donna Ikenberry/Animals Animals/Earth Scenes; P74 Bruno Herdt/Getty Image, Inc./Photo Disc, Inc.; P79 Michael Thompson/Animals Animals/Earth Scenes; P80 br Mark C. Burnett/Photo Researchers, Inc.; P80 l Wil Blanche/Omni-Photo Communications; P80 tr David Parker/Science Photo Library/Photo Researchers, Inc.; P82 Barbara K. Hesse/Visuals Unlimited, Inc.; P83 Barbara K. Hesse/Visuals Unlimited, Inc.; P84 Barbara K. Hesse/Visuals Unlimited, Inc.

Chapter 4: P85 Jim Zuckerman/Corbis; P86 l David Julian/Phototake; P86 r Stuart Westmorland/Photo Researchers, Inc.; P87 Andrew Syred/SPL/Science Photo Library/Photo Researchers, Inc.; P88 Jim Steinberg/Photo Researchers, Inc.; P89 Bob Daemmrich/Stock, Boston, Inc.; P92 b Richard Shiell/Animals Animals/Earth Scenes; P92 t Rod Planck/Photo Researchers, Inc.; P93 Hank Morgan/Photo Researchers, Inc.; P94 bl John Spragens, Jr./Photo Researchers, Inc.; P94 br Fred Whitehead/Animals Animals/Earth Scenes; P94 mr Eastcott/Momatiuk/Animals Animals/Earth Scenes; P94 tr Bruce Watkins/Animals Animals/Earth Scenes; P95 b Jim Brandenburg/Minden Pictures; P95 t Stephen Ingram/Animals Animals/Earth Scenes; P98 col. 1 Carson Baldwin, Jr./Animals Animals/Earth Scenes; P98 col. 2 C. C. Lockwood/Animals Animals/Earth Scenes; P98 col. 3 Johnny Johnson/DRK Photo; P98 col. 4 E. R. Degginger/Animals Animals/Earth Scenes; P99 Fogden, M. OSF/Animals Animals/Earth Scenes; P101 NASA/Science Photo Library/Photo Researchers, Inc.; P102 John Lemker/Animals Animals/Earth Scenes; P104 Jim Brandenburg/Minden Pictures; P105 b E. R. Degginger/Color-Pic, Inc.; P105 t NASA/Goddard Space Flight Center/Science Photo Library/Photo Researchers, Inc.; P106 b Keith Kent/Science Photo Library/Photo Researchers, Inc.; P106 t Mary Evans Picture Library; P107 National Severe Storms Laboratory/Color-Pic, Inc.; P112 Jim Zuckerman/Corbis; P113 Jim Zuckerman/Corbis; P114 Jim Zuckerman/Corbis

Chapter 5: P115 Kevin Schafer/Peter Arnold, Inc.; P115 inset Manfred Kage/Peter Arnold, Inc.; P117 Wolfgang Kaehler/Corbis; P118 Michael T. Stubben/Visuals Unlimited, Inc.; P119 Frans Lanting/Minden Pictures; P122 l John Lemker/Animals Animals/Earth Scenes; P122 r Reuters NewMedia Inc./Corbis; P126 Phyllis Greenberg/Animals Animals/Earth Scenes; P127 Robert Lubeck/Animals Animals/Earth Scenes; P127 inset Inga Spence/Visuals Unlimited, Inc.; P128 b Andy Deering/Omni-Photo Communications, Inc.; P128 m Francois Gohier/Photo Researchers, Inc.; P128 t David McNew/Peter Arnold, Inc.; P129 b Tomas D. W. Friedmann/Photo Researchers, Inc.; P129 tl Dan Guravich/Photo Researchers, Inc.; P129 tm Charlie Ott/Photo Researchers, Inc.; P129 tr Bios (Compost-Visage)/Peter Arnold, Inc.; P130 Kevin Schafer/Peter Arnold, Inc.; P131 Kevin Schafer/Peter Arnold, Inc.; P132 Kevin Schafer/Peter Arnold, Inc.